Southold Connections

Historical and Biographical Sketches of Northeastern Long Island

by
Judy Jacobson

CLEARFIELD

Reprinted for
Clearfield Company, Inc. by
Genealogical Publishing Co., Inc.
Baltimore, Maryland
1992, 1997

Printed in 1991 for Clearfield Company Inc.,
by Genealogical Publishing Company, Inc., Baltimore, MD

International Standard Book Number: 0-8063-1303-X

Made in the United States of America

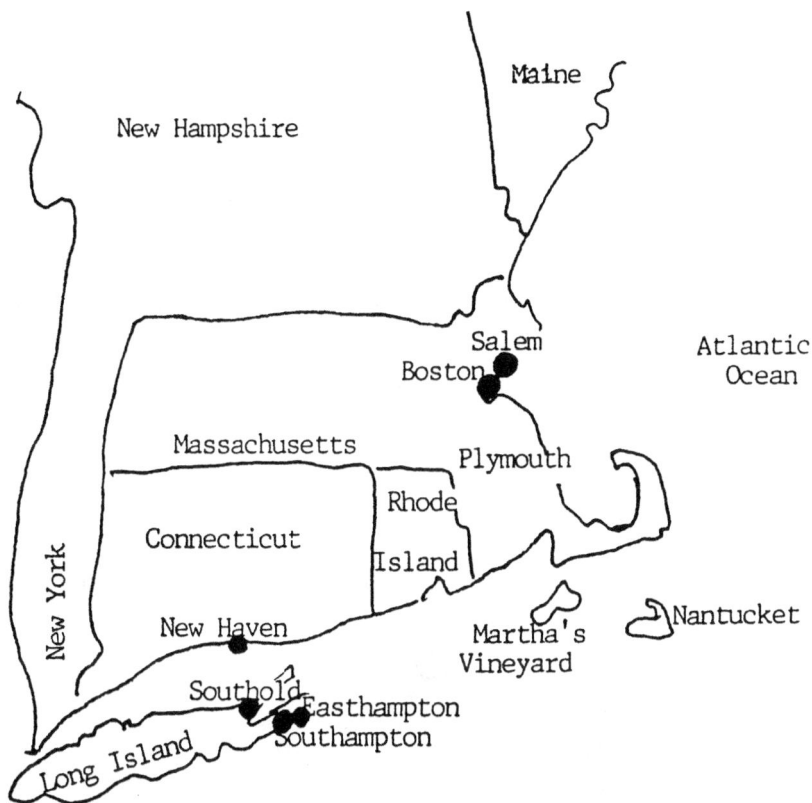

Maine

New Hampshire

Atlantic
Ocean

Salem
Boston

Massachusetts

Plymouth

Rhode

Connecticut

Island

New York

New Haven

Nantucket

Martha's
Vineyard

Southold
Easthampton
Southampton

Long Island

NEW ENGLAND, CIRCA 1675

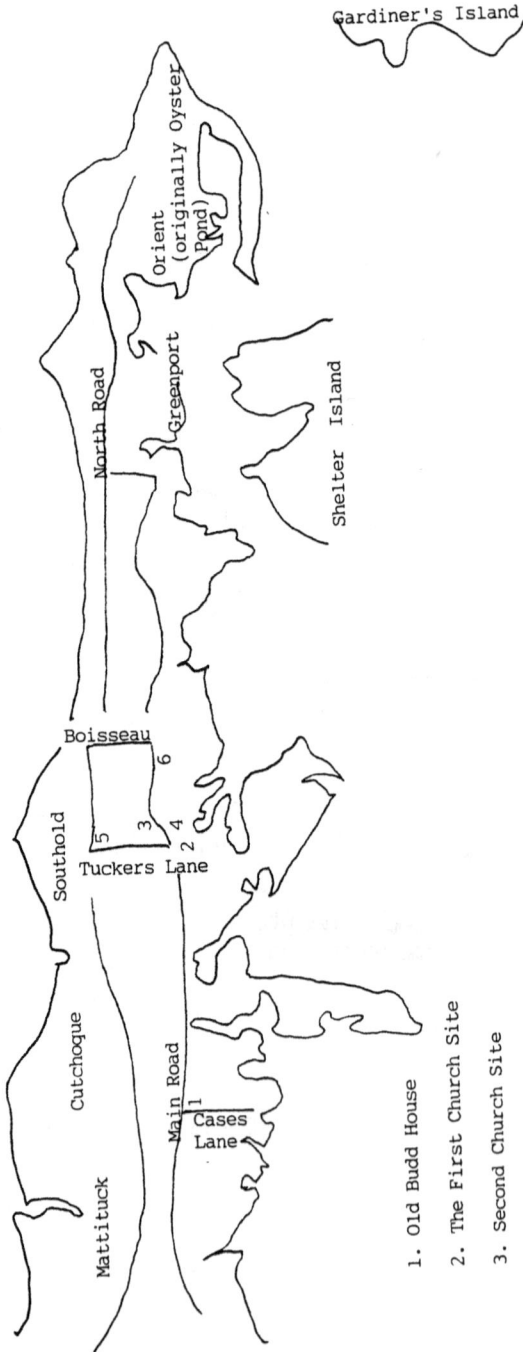

Gardiner's Island

Long Island Sound

Orient (originally Oyster Pond)

North Road

Greenport

Shelter Island

Boisseau

Southold

Tuckers Lane

Cutchoque

Mattituck

Main Road

Cases Lane

1. Old Budd House

2. The First Church Site

3. Second Church Site

4. Third Church Site

5. Second Budd House

6. Thomas Moore House

Table of Contents

Preface

Through the years I was growing up, I heard various stories about my ancestors. I never paid much attention to them.

But then I had children of my own and suddenly I wanted to pass on our heritage to them. My great-aunt gave me the family Bible and some very old pictures. My mother dug out the long saved papers and retold the stories I had heard before, but had never really listened to. And the information began to build up.

A distant cousin wrote a genealogy about one of the families, giving bits and pieces about related families. I began writing others searching for the same names. They led me to more people. I wrote to libraries and town historians. We visited the towns in which my ancestors had lived. And the information built up.

And suddenly, people were writing me asking for help. The more information I had, the more people wrote seeking help.

I answered every single letter - making mounds of photocopies and writing reams of paper to answer their questions. The more information I had, the more complicated and timely the answers.

It honestly got to the point I dreaded going to the mailbox. While I continued to answer all queries completely, the chore of searching through all my files for the answers got terribly time consuming.

A friend and fellow genealogist suggested I write up all I had on each family. Then when a query arrived, I could just photocopy the appropriate family and send it. It made sense. I did want to help others, but simply did not have the time to answer all the questions fully.

So I began to write. As I began putting it all together, I found I had more information then even I had realized. I had enough information on the Southold families for a small book.

But in the beginning it was Todd and Jodi Jacobson who gave me the inspiration. It was Arlene Mathieson, my mother, and Ruth Weller, my great-aunt, who gave me the basics on which to build.

It was Betty Brassington who unselfishly shared information when I wrote that first query letter. It was Truman Landon, the distant cousin, who wrote a book about the Landons that gave me so many clues to follow.

It was Magdaline Goodrich, the Southold Town Historian, who added so much information. It was Ruth Cheney Ryan who, like myself, was trying to do New England research from Mississippi. It was Walter Winans, Bert Barker and Craig Hamilton who unselfishly shared information. It was Sue Snow who talked me into writing it all down. And it was the helpful librarians at Southold Free Library.

They did so much and I thank them all.

But most of all, it was my husband, Harry Jacobson, who made this book possible. My loving thanks to him

      - for picking up the tab for a trip to Southold and the National Archives and all the other places we've gone to search;

      - for entertaining the kids while mom spent hours in the library;

      - for combing the cemeteries with me, trying to read illegible tombstones;

      - and for being patient while I "played" with my genealogy evening after evening.

Judy Jacobson

Symbols Used

aft	after a certain date
b.	born
betw	between two dates
bro	brother of
by	by a certain date
c.	circa (approximately)
d.	died
dau	daughter of
m.	married
m1.	married first
m2.	married second
r.	resided
sis	sister of
wid	widow of
1670/1	old calendar
1670-71	between two dates

It began with King James and his assaults on social and religious liberties in England It ended with the English Civil War. During the years between, life became so difficult many people left England for the New World and the freedom it promised.

The church begun by Henry VIII, while broken away from the Roman Church, had maintained many Catholic similarities. Under Elizabeth I, reformers sought to "purify" the Anglican Church of its "popish elements". During the Stuart reigns, many formed churches more closely associated with Calvinist or Presbyterian forms while steadfastly maintaining their allegiance to the Church of England. But Charles I issued edicts against the purifiers and, in 1626, he announced he would "not admit of the least innovation in the matter of doctrine, or the discipline of the church." But the "purifiers" or Puritans firmly believed Roman Catholics were too strong in Charles I's court. His queen was a French Roman Catholic and William Laud, who became the Archbishop of Canterbury in 1633, called Puritans "the most dangerous enemies of the state". In addition, many of Charles' subjects were outraged when he allied England with Spain, a Catholic country, against Sweden and the Netherlands, Protestant countries.

Religious difficulties were not the only problems faced by the Puritans. In <u>Ideas in America</u>, Grob and Beck stated that Puritan emphasis on industry and enterprise appealed to the middle class in a way that it could not appeal to the peasantry or nobility. That same capitalistic emphasis gave those opposing changes in the Anglican Church a weapon to use against the Puritans; bringing economic as well as social, political and religious consequences. Miller, in <u>This New Man, the American</u>, stated that during the reigns of Elizabeth I, James I and Charles I, "monopolies covering most of the articles in common use in England were granted to court favorites and wealthy merchants". Monopolies were granted to protect vital industries. But with monopolies allowed in everything from buttons to salmon, prices soared. Religious and economic policies pursued by the first two Stuart kings hardened opposition in Parliament, and made Puritans the leaders of the opposition. Miller proposed that the mixing of politics and economics produced the depression that followed -a depression felt mostly by Puritans in the textile industry.

Unable to change the Anglican Church, the economic suffering and the religious persecution; the Puritans chose to leave England. While Charles I did not usually help Puritans, his need for revenue overrode his religious prejudices. With money as his prime motivation, Charles granted the Puritans a charter in New England. Charles may have also felt some of his problems would be over once the bothersome Puritans were far away in the New World.

But was religious freedom the primary reason for the massive emigration of the early 1600's? In <u>Fathers of New England</u>, Andrews cited lack of land and poor social conditions along with a restlessness and discontent in England as the chief factors for those who emigrated. While religion has been thought to be the major factor of the mass emigration to the New

World, Andrews claimed less then one-fifth of those in Massachusetts in the early 1600's were Christians.

But in <u>This New Man, the American</u>, Miller argued that if economics had been the primary consideration, the Puritans "would not have trusted themselves to the hazards of the sea and the even greater perils of the wilderness." While they knew God would see them through the hardships they knew awaited them, they would not expect God to give his blessing to "a mere real-estate venture."

For Rev. John Youngs there seems to be very little doubt that religious freedom was the reason he left his home in Southwold, England, to set out for Salem, Massachusetts which had been settled after the break-up of the Cape Anne trading post. From 1624-28, settlers from Dorset, Somerset and Devon arrived in "Naumkeag" (Salem). On his arrival, Rev. Youngs discovered others fleeing England like himself, had created an abundance of ministers and teachers in Salem. Finally, Youngs moved his band of eleven followers and their families to what would become Southold, Long Island.

Osterweiss, in <u>Three Centuries in New Haven, 1638-1938</u>, suggested that "New Haveners persuaded them to settle Southold." Thompson, in <u>History of Long Island</u>, wrote "The governor of New Haven and the magistrates there, not only aided the settlers in their negotiations for the purchase of the soil, but actually took the conveyance in their own names." In a way, Trumbell agreed in <u>History of Connecticut</u>. When he wrote, "It also appears that New Haven, or their confederates, purchased and settled Yennycock (Southold) on Long Island." But Trumbell and Thompson erroneously reported that Pastor Young had been a minister in Hingham, England, and he emigrated with some of his church members, and settled in New Haven. Trumbell claimed the group left New Haven because, not being members of the colony, they were unable to hold office or become freemen. Research showed the founders of Southold emigrated at various times and from various parts of England, making it impossible to have come from one church.

Those eleven settlers with Rev. John Youngs were William Wells, Peter Hallock, John Tuthill, Richard Terry, Thomas Mapes, Mathias Corbin, Robert Ackerly, Jacob Cory, John Conklin, Isaac Arnold and John Budd. With the exception of Hallock, all had their families with them.

In 1635, Long Island had been assigned by the Council of New England to William Alexander, Earl of Stirling. According to Osterweiss, New Haven merchants acquired it from the Earl in 1640. Then, on December 13, 1640, nine Shennecock Indians gave their deed to the eastern tip of Long Island, including two narrow peninsulas divided by a forty mile long body of water. That deed was finally acknowledged on November 24, 1686. Although the island had been given to the Virginia Company of Plymouth, the citizens of New Haven considered it theirs.

As Miller explained in <u>This New Man, the American</u>, every adult male was a landowner, unlike in England. When a new town was organized, each inhabitant was allotted land according to his family size and/or wealth.

A 1650 Dutch report listed thirty homes in Southold. A 1652 town meeting record indicated homes were built of logs with small oil covered windows and thatched roofs. According to Selah Youngs, each householder was required to have a ladder which reached the top of his house as fire protection. By 1660 there were at least fifty lots with those types of dwellings in Southold.

According to J.H. French's Historical and Statistical Gazetteer of New York State, the first church of Southold was New York's first church structure. Founded October 21, 1640, the church looked more like a fortress and was probably constructed of rough frame or logs with a dirt floor. It served as church, town hall and fortress before eventually becoming a jail when the court ordered a place "for the punishment and safekeeping of prisoners." Samuel Youngs and Thomas Clarke were the carpenters hired to appraise the meeting house for conversion to a county jail.

The second church; built in 1683, the year Suffolk County was organized; was located across Main Street from the original church. The cornerstone for the third church was laid in 1803. The Puritans who were members of that church were, in reality, Presbyterians.

In 1643, New Haven, founded by John Davenport; Stamford; Southold; Milford; and Guilford united to make the New Haven Colony. The Colony was merely a confederation with each town responsible for its own affairs. Southold remained the only Long Island town in the colony. In 1648, Southold became a member of the courts of New Haven, where jury trials were deemed unnecessary because judges found the answers in the Bible.

Southold adopted a theocratic government based on New Haven's form, with church membership mandatory to vote and hold office. According to Thompson, an appointed committee regulated the admission of new settlers. No one could become an inhabitant without its approval: no one could sell or lease his house or land to an unapproved stranger. The Mosaic Code became the law. The sole right of church members to vote did not last long. French wrote, "in 1657 the Mosaic Code was superseded by one better adapted to the circumstances of the people" The government was run by town meetings which began at 8 a.m. Each man had a vote. According to Albertson Case's Historical Sketch of Southold Town, the quarterly town meeting was considered so important that a twenty shilling fine was fixed on anyone not attending. A constable was the chief executive official and elected overseers conducted town affairs. Appointed magistrates came later. Lt. John Budd and Corporal Barnabas Wines headed the militia in the early years.

Southold remained under New Haven's jurisdiction until 1662, when the town united with Connecticut and sent representatives to it's General Court. Osterweiss wrote that "inhabitants of Southold there long resentful at New Haven's limited franchise, transferred their allegiance to Connecticut." Suffolk became a county on November 1, 1683, and occupied the eastern two-thirds of Long Island. Southold was recognized as a town on March 7, 1788. Riverhead was removed from the township in 1792.

Despite their organization, the settlers faced several problems. Although the Indians were friendly, according to Case, "it was ordered lawful for any inhabitant finding any Indian with gun or bows and arrows or dogs anywhere between

Arshamomogue and Plum Gut to detain and bring him before the proper authorities. This proceeded from their fear of loss among their cattle and swine then pasturing." The Indians used tame wolves as dogs so Indian dogs were considered dangerous.

In later years Indians became servants or slaves of the whites before disappearing altogether. The last pure Sachem of the Montauks, Stephen Tankhouse, died circa 1875, according to Youngs. Tankhouse was descended from Wyandauch, the Montauk's Sachem during Rev. John Youngs' time.

Long Island east of the Wading River, and Shelter and Robins Islands had been controlled by the Shennecock, Montauk, Manhansett and Corchanug Indian tribes. The four chiefs were brothers who, on the whole, were usually friendly with the settlers. Although the Montauks were the most numerous and powerful of the tribes, the Naraganssetts caused most of Southold's Indian problems. Patrols set up for protection from the Indians continued until after King Philip's War, circa 1675-77. A militia formed under a 1643 article of the United Colonies consisted of all males ages sixteen to sixty. Anyone who did not furnish his own gun, sword, powder, matches, flints and bullets had to pay a 10 shilling fine for default. They had six training days a year and a review each quarter.

Another problem facing the community was the Quakers. Severe laws were passed against Quakers and defending one was a fineable offense. Criticism of a magistrate or minister by a Quaker or anyone defending Quaker rights was punishable by a whipping or heavy fine, as several Southold residents discovered. But the problem was not limited to Southold. Hoffman, in Pathways to Freedom, reported that America's first book burning occurred when the Boston town council ordered the burning of Quaker tracts. Although Quakers were characterized as "a cursed Sect of Heretiacks" by the New Haven Colony. Yet several Southold residents joined the sect.

A bigger problem for the settlers were the Dutch who also claimed the land. In 1636, Jacobus Van Corlaer was given the first Dutch patent for land on Long Island. And in 1640, the Dutch had made a formal purchase of Long Island. So when the English settled in the Southold area, the Dutch felt their land had been seized by the English.

A 1650 treaty signed in Hartford supposedly fixed a boundary between the English and Dutch claims, with towns east of the boundary falling under Connecticut jurisdiction. However, in 1664, Connecticut claimed all of Long Island.

To complicate matters more, Capt. John Scott tried to acquire Long Island for himself by helping the Duke of York conquer New Netherlands. Scott was arrested and imprisoned for his role by Connecticut, but the Duke of York received the patent making him proprietor of Long Island along with other parts of New York, Connecticut, New Jersey, Martha's Vineyard, and Nantucket.

For a short while during the last Anglo-Dutch War, the Dutch controlled northern Long Island, including Southampton, Easthampton and Southold. However, the towns and nearby islands were never really under and never accepted Dutch rule. Although Dutch naval ships captured vessels from these towns, Dutch officers never demanded forfeitures. And none of the Dutch acts were ever enforced.

The Peace of Westminster, signed on February 19, 1674, ended the Anglo-Dutch Wars and returned all captured land to the original owners, establishing Long Island as part of the English colonies. The treaty also encouraged Southampton, Easthampton and Southold to declare themselves under Connecticut rule.

As the treaty was being signed, Fritz-John Winthrop and fifty of his men went to Southold to uphold Connecticut's claim. Late that February, four vessels of Dutch soldiers arrived. After a short battle, the Dutch forces, despite their advantage in numbers, left and never returned.

History also left behind some mysteries and lore concerning the North Fork of the island. In 1690, William Kidd was an established sea captain, shipowner and property owner in New York City. Originally a legitimate privateer commissioned by William III of Great Britain and financed by wealthy Englishmen including the Earl of Bellomont, Captain Kidd's contract stipulated he and his men were paid only when he secured a pirate ship. Unable to do so, Kidd turned to pirating himself. In April, 1699, in the West Indies, Kidd discovered he had been denounced as a pirate. He sailed for New York, taking shelter in Oyster Bay, Long Island near Southold, while he tried to persuade Bellomont, the Colonial governor, that he was innocent. Kidd claimed his men had locked him up while they committed piracies. Bellomont, refusing to listen, sent Kidd to England where he was tried and found guilty of murdering a crew member and of five counts of piracy. Captain Kidd was executed in 1701. Later some of his booty was discovered on Gardiner's Island, just east of Southold, leading to speculation that yet more of Captain Kidd's treasure might still be buried in the area.

The sea has obviously had a great influence on the area. Through the years, collecting oysters and clams, plentiful in the sea around Long Island; shipbuilding; whaling; and fishing were the principle occupations of the inhabitants along the shore.

The south shore of Long Island has small irregular bays while the northern coast is straight, except for 2 or 3 inlets. But sandbars located a distance from the shore wrecked havoc with ships. In the 1860 <u>Historical and Statistical Gazetteer of New York</u>, French wrote, "The traveler along the beach is seldom out of sight of wrecks". Between November 1, 1854 and June 28, 1857, "5 ships, 9 barks, 16 brigs, 25 schooners, and 9 sloops were wrecked, or in distress off this coast". Southold sent many of her men to the sea: many never returned. French also reported that Greenport near Southold had 7 whaling, 100 fishing and 102 small licensed vessels in 1890. While whaling was originally done in open boats near shore; eventually, larger vessels were sent all the way to the poles.

In addition to fishing and whaling vessels, the waters around Southold were filled with large ships carrying goods. Just prior to the American Revolution, Long Island Sound was filled with ships as New York City became a major port and distribution center.

And when the American Revolution arrived, Long Island, despite it's remoteness, was not left out. On August 22, 1776, General Israel Putnam's outmaneuvered and inexperienced recruits panicked during the Battle of Long Island. Luckily, fog and rain aided George Washington's escape, first to Manhattan Island and, finally into Pennsylvania while British troops were in close pursuit.

The Battle of Long Island took place primarily on the opposite end of Long Island. But in November, 1780, Southold found itself in the midst of the war. Catherine Crary, in The Price of Loyalty, presented a newspaper account of the battle as reported in New York's "Royal Gazette". According to the account, about eighty rebels and officers formerly from Long Island, crossed Long Island Sound from New Haven, landing near the Wading River of Southold, and hid in the area for several days assisted by old friends. While some were left behind to guard the boats, about fifty rebels crossed to the southern end of the island where they found Loyalist refugees. In the insuing battle, many Loyalists were wounded or killed. Forty Loyalists were taken prisoner.

During the war, small craft on each side launched raids on Long Island Sound which Bruce Lancaster, in The American Heritage Book of the Revolution, said had "no bearing on the course of the war". But still that "fringe-warfare went on, savage and bloody".

Today the northern, shorter peninsula of eastern Long Island is the township of Southold. The village of Southold is near the south shore and in the approximate middle of the township, 100 miles from New York City.

Chapter 1

Brockett Family

John
    d. November, 1690
    Children
        Grace? (see below)
        Mary - bapt. September 26 or 28, 1646; New Haven
            m. Ephraim Pennington, 1690
            r. Wallingford
        John - bapt. December 31, 1642
        Befruitful - bapt. February 23, 1644
        Benjamin - bapt. February 23, 1644
        Silence - bapt. June 3, 1648
        Abigail - bapt. March 24, 1650
        Samuel - bapt. January 16, 1651

Grace
    b. by 1666
    m. John Vail, by 1681
    d. May 18, 1751
    Children
        Abigail
        Josiah - b.c. 1693
        Irene
        Daniel - b.c. 1694
        Tabitha
        Samuel - b.c. 1696
        John - m. Hannah Landon
        James - d. September 9, 1675; Albany, New York
        Mary - m. 1707
        Benjamin - b. 1706
            m. Mary Paine
        Obadiah

   The last name of Grace's family has been given as Hallock,
Braddick, Burgess and Brockett. Brockett appears to be the most
likely. Most genealogies have made no attempt to identify Grace
in anyway accept by the name the author has decided to assign
her and by mentioning that she was the daughter of John, a sea
captain who lived on the western half of a lot owned by Lt. John
Budd in Southold.

   It is possible that John was related to the John Brockett
of originally Saxon ancestry whose family has been traced to the
1200's, according to the <u>Directory of the Heads of New England
Families</u>. Brockett Hall, the ancestral home, was in
Wheathampstead, Co. Hert.(see Appendix I). Ancestors in that
Brockett line included Sir John Brockett who was knighted by
Edward VI in 1546. Another Brockett family resided in Westleton
and Bramfield in Suffolk Co., England, near Rev. John Young's
ancestral home.

   According to Mary Louise Marshall Hutton, compiler of
<u>Seventeenth Century Colonial Ancestors,</u> John Brockett was born
in 1609 and died in November 1690. However, that would mean
that he still had not married at age 32 and that he was 33 years
old before his first child was born. While, of course, that's
possible, a later birth date would make more sense.

   No matter what his birth year was, John Brockett can be
linked directly to both the New Haven Colony and to John Budd of

Southold. On June 26, 1637, a John Brockett arrived in the New World aboard the "Hector" with John Budd and others from London parishes. According to <u>History of the New Haven Colony</u>, John Brockett signed the first covenant at New Haven, in 1639 and was assigned the last seat in the 6th row "on the other side of the door" of New Haven's meeting house on March 10, 1647/8. He was listed in 1641 town records as having only one person in his family, owning approximately 200 acres and paying 2 shillings 6 pence of tax per year. His daughter Mary was baptized in New Haven on September 28, 1646. She married Ephraim Pennington.

In early summer, 1638, John Brockett was a surveyor and directed the staking out of New Haven's town plots. He reserved the center section of nine square sections for a marketplace. In addition, Brockett added two suburbs. John Budd, later of Southold, received one of the town lots.

Years later (circa 1667), according to <u>Three Centuries of New Haven</u>, those attending a New Haven town meeting heard a request from John Brockett, then of Wallingford. In response, selectmen were instructed to listen to "this Elder Statesman" concerning his ideas for planning roads.

So a John Brockett was active in the area, and had connections with people in Southold. Grace might well have been his daughter, or the daughter of his son John (b. 1642). One of them may even have lived in Southold between the 1647 date which last put him in New Haven and the 1660's when he was living in Wallingford.

Of the other possible surnames for Grace, Burgess and Braddick were not common in the area. The Hallock name was the only other viable possibility. However, no John Hallock could be found who would have been old enough to be Grace's father. And none of the possible fathers, including John Brockett, were sea captains.

Most sources have agreed Grace's father's name was John. They also agree her father lived on half of a lot owned by John Budd. Depending upon the source, either John Hallock or John Cory purchased one-half of the John Budd house in 1678. John Budd III was a ship's captain. That supported the possibility of John Hallock as Grace's father. However, the other half of the house was purchased by Grace's brother-in-law, Jeremiah Vail, Jr. Jeremiah was named for his father, Grace's father-in-law. Could those who put Grace's father in John Budd's house have meant to place her father-in-law in it instead?

Whatever her last name, Grace was born by 1666 and married John Vail of Southold by 1681. On July 18, 1684; she signed a deed with her parents-in-law, Jeremiah and Joyce Vail, and her husband John. Grace died May 18, 1751.

Chapter 2
Part 1

Brown(e) Families
The Richard Browne Family

Richard
    d. October 16, 1655
    Children
        Richard (see below)

Richard II (Lt.)
    m. Hannah King
    d. 1688; Suffolk Co., Long Island
    Children
        Richard (see below)
        Jonathan - b.c. 1653
            m. Elizabeth, dau of Captain Nathaniel Sylvester
            of Shelter Island, New York.
            d. August 19, 1710

Richard III (Ensign)
    m. Dorothy King
    Children
        Richard (see below)
        Samuel - b. March 21, 1686
            m1. Mary (c. 1691-1711)
            m2. Rebecca, dau of Samuel and Elizabeth Rogers
            Beebe; January 14, 1712/13

Richard IV (Capt.)
    b. April, 1683; Southold, Long Island
    m. Anne, dau of Christopher Young III; February 21, 1704/5;
    Southold, Long Island
    d. between 1765-1771; Southold, Long Island
    Children
        Christopher - b. June 29, 1714
            d. August 25, 1739
        Richard - b. November 21, 1708
            m. Hannah Hawke
            d. September 23, 1776
            Children
                Anna - b. April 30, 1745
                    d. August 13, 1753
        Anne - b. January 6, 1705/6
            d. September 29, 1729
        Henry - b. January 12, 1710/11; Southold, Long Island
            m. Mary Paine (1712-1742); November 25, 1731;
            Southampton, Long Island
            will proved - February 14, 1774; Southold, Long
            Island
            Children
                Paine - b. 1742; Southold Long Island
                    m. Ann Halsey; c. 1771; Southold, Long
                    Island
                    d. December, 1812; Chester, New York
        Mehetable - b.c. 1695
            d. August 26, 1712
        Peter - b. September 11, 1719
            d. June 4, 1747
        Dorothy - d. aft. 1747
        Daughter - b. November 18, 1707
            d. November 22, 1707

12

Several Brown/Browne families were involved with early Southold, Long Island. One was the family of Richard Browne. One of the Richard Brownes above may have been the one who sailed aboard the "Mary and John" from London to New England leaving March 24, 1663. Or he may have been the Richard Browne who was made a freeman of Connecticut in 1662. A Richard Browne was bound to a Thomas Moore (the name of a prominent Southold, Long Island resident) for four years. That Richard Browne arrived in New England aboard the ship "Saphire Ketch" (sic) in March, 1679. Richard II in the genealogy above might have been any of these Richard Brownes.

In Suffolk County Wills, a January 19, 1661 inventory of a Richard Browne's goods was reported. The inventory was done by Abraham Browne and Thomas Clark and his estate was valued at 80 pounds 18 shillings 12 pence.

Chapter 2
Part 2

The Simon Browne Family

Simon
    b.c. 1540; Lancaster, England
    Children
        Thomas (see below)

Thomas
    Children
        Francis (see below)

Francis
    b. Brandon, Suffolk Co,. England
    d. May 9, 1626; Suffolk Co. England
    Children
        William (see below)

William
    b. March 1, 1608
    m1. Mary, dau of Christopher Youngs of Southwold, England
    m2. Sarah, dau of Samuel Smith of Yarmouth
    d. January 20, 1688; Salem, Massachusetts
    Children
        William (see below)
        John - b. October, 1641
                d. 1669
        Samuel - b. July 31, 1644
        Benjamin - b. 1648
                m. Mary, dau of Rev. John Hicks
                d. December 7, 1708
        Sarah - b. December 23, 1649
                m. Thomas Deane, 1665
        Joseph - m. Mehitable, dau of Gov. William Brenton
                d. May 9, 1678; Charlestown, Massachusetts
        Mary - m. Walt Winthrop
                d. June 14, 1690
        James

William II
    b. April 14, 1639
    m1. Hannah, dau of George Curwin; December 29, 1664
    m2. Rebecca Bayley; April 26, 1694
    d. February 14 or 23, 1716
    Children
        Samuel (see below)
        William (1st) - b. 1666
                d. by 1671
        Hannah - b. March 16, 1668
        William (2nd) - b. September 5, 1671
        John - b. November 2, 1672
        Sarah - b. December 10, 1674
                d. c. 1688
        Mary - b. August 22, 1679
                m. Justice Benjamin Lynde

Samuel
    b. October 8, 1669
    m1. Eunice Turner
    m2. Abigail, dau of John Kech or Keach of Bristol; February
    22, 1706

```
d. June, 1731
Children
     William - b.c. 1709
          d. April 27, 1763
     Samuel
     Benjamin
```

The earliest Browne traced of this family was Simon Browne of Browne Hall, Lancashire County, England. It is believed he later moved to Brandon, Suffolk County.

His son Thomas had Francis Browne I of Wybred Hall, Brandon on the "Lit Ouse River" (Little Ouse River) in Suffolk Co. England. Francis died in Suffolk on May 9, 1626, the year John Endicott and fifty emigrants arrived in Salem and Pieter Minuit landed at Manhattan in the New World. A Francis Browne, perhaps his son, died in New Haven in 1668. The New Haven Francis left an April 13, 1668 will with bequests to sons Samuel, Ebenezer, John and Eleazer; to daughter Lydia; and wife Mary. In 1723, James Landon of Southold, Long Island married Mary Wilmont, daughter of a Francis Browne. While Mary could not have been the daughter of either of the above Francis Brownes; she may have been a descendent through the Francis Browne who circa 1715 was skipper and part owner of the "Speedwell".

Francis I of Wybred Hall had a son, William, who was born on March 1, 1608. William was an apprentice to a merchant in Southwold, England, before emigrating. His wife, Mary, daughter of Christopher and Margaret Youngs, and he arrived in Salem in 1635, probably aboard the "Love". William was 26 years old.

According to Hotten, their July 13, 1635 emigration notation was written, "Theis vnder-written names are to be transported to New England imbarqued in the 'Love' Joseph Young Mr." for "fisherman Willm Browne 26" and "Mary Browne 26". Savage stated William was probably a member of the Fishmongers Co. Mary died in 1637 in Salem. William married second Sarah, daughter of Samuel Smith.

In 1641, William became a freeman. According to the Massachusetts Bay Co. charter, all adult males in the colony might be entitled to be a freeman and guaranteed the right to vote. The original Massachusetts Bay Co. imagined only stockholders should have that right. But changing the charter to a constitution limited stockholder's rights. So Winthrop extended the suffrage to include all adult male church members. Eventually non-church members were given the right.

William was a representative in 1654, 1659 and 1666; and assistant from 1680-83. He died January 20, 1688. His will was dated March 12, 1687 and was filed in Suffolk Co. with bequests to his family; friends; the church; Mr. Higginson, his pastor; the poor; the school; and the college, to pay for "poor scholars". He gave his daughter Mary Winthrop the "biggest balcer", the "silver tankard and six of the silver spoons". He also mentioned his daughter "Browne". So at least one daughter had not married by the time of his death. John Hawthorne witnessed the will.

Another son, Joseph, graduated from Harvard College in 1666. He was granted a fellowship but resigned it on September 16, 1673 in order to become an ordained preacher.

According to Savage, son Benjamin married Mary Hicks, daughter of Rev. John Hicks, a non-conformist English minister. Benjamin was town representative in 1693 and 1699 and a member of the Executive Council from 1702 to 1705. He was a large benefactor to Harvard College.

Yet another son, William II, was born April 14, 1639. He married Hannah Curwin. Hannah died November 21, 1692 and on April 26, 1694, William II married Rebecca Bayley. He was made freeman in 1665 and a member of the Andros Council from 1687-89. In addition to being a representative, he was a counsellor under a charter of William and Mary and a member of the Council of Safety in 1689. He died February 14 or 23, 1716. His daughter, Mary, married Chief Justice Benjamin Lynde.

Col. Samuel Browne was a counsellor and judge. He married, first, Eunice Turner and, second, Abigail Kech or Keach. Samuel had at least three sons - Samuel, Benjamin, and William. William graduated from Harvard college in 1727. And another William Browne served on the Massachusetts Supreme Court.

Chapter 3

Budd Family

John I
 m. Kate Bond or Howe by 1599
 Children
  John (see below)

John II
 bapt. 1599; Stepney, England
 m. Katherine Brown(e)
 d. 1678, Long Island
 Children
  John (see below)
  Jane - m. Joseph Horton
  Anna - m. Benjamin Horton
  Joshua

John III
 b. 1620; Stepney, England
 will proved - October, 1684
 Children
  Marie (see below)
  Hannah - m. Jonathan Hart(t)
  John - m. Molly Horton, Long Island
  Joseph
  Ann

Marie (Mary)
 b. September, 1654; Southold, Long Island
 m. Christopher Youngs II, 1675
 d. 1723/24; Southold, Long Island

  The Budd (also spelled "Bird", "Bud", and "Budde") family
of Southold may have been descendents of Jean "Budde" who left
Normandy with William the Conquerer in 1066. According to
Lyon's Memorial, Vol. 3, Jean Budde was made the Earl of Essex.
Although the lineage was described for five and one-half
centuries, only four generations were listed after Jean 1 -
William 2, Richard 3, John 4, and John 5 who married Katherine
Browne. Obviously not enough generations were given to cover
over five centuries.

  Little information was available about the first John Budd
(number 4 in Lyon's Memorial). His son was baptized in 1599 in
Stepney, England. Stepney, a district in the borough of Tower
Hamlets, is two miles east of London Bridge. The Thames River
is on its southern border and Whitechapel is on its west.

  A John "Bird" was named in William Ambrose's 1637 will
found in Genealogical Gleanings in England. Ambrose, a clerk
from Stepney, willed money owed to him by "Bird" and his wife to
his sister Cicely and his brother Peter. Peter's 1653 will
mentioned his wife Judith and her son, John "Bird". Judith's
former husband had an estate in the Chester area, according to
Peter's will. However, Peter mentioned others who he noted "are
now in New England". That notation was not added to his mention
of John "Bird".

  The John in this genealogy married Kate. Since John I and
John II were co-administrators of a Howe estate in England, Kate
may have been a Howe.

In <u>The New Haven Colony</u>; John II, christened in 1599 in Stepney, England; was listed with John and Elizabeth Davenport's group to America on the second sailing of the "Hector". Most of those who went were from "St. Antholins" parish of London, St. Lawrences parish of Old Jewry, or St. Stephens of Coleman Street, London, and their surrounding neighborhoods.

John II married Katherine Brown(e) in England. She may have been a relative of William Browne of Southwold, England, who married Mary, sister of Joseph and Rev. John Youngs, and went to Salem on Capt. Joseph Youngs ship, the "Love". Children born to Katherine and John Budd II included Jane, Anna, Joshua and John III.

Budd was a planter in the New Haven Colony (1639) where he later was listed as a representative (1643) and court deputy (1653). Southold was part of the New Haven Colony. He also was a lieutenant of Southold's Training Band (by 1654), a judge in Southold (1657), and a deputy to the Connecticut legislature (1664).

In April, 1641, John was listed in <u>The History of the New Haven Colony</u> as having six persons in his family. His estate was worth 110 pounds (one of the lesser amounts) and he owned 193.5 acres.

He built his first known home in the woodlands of Southold in 1649. It had a medieval feeling with a steep roof, small windows with leaded panes and a large chimney stack. There were two rooms on each floor with two fireplaces over nine feet wide, three feet deep, and five feet high, back to back.

After a 1658 trip to Antiqua where he became fascinated with homes of Antiqua planters, John Budd built another home in the same style on the west end of Southold's main road. Since John Budd was becoming wealthier and even developing an association with the English King, he was able to use some of the largest trees on Long Island. He gave the first house to his daughter and her husband, Benjamin Horton, as a wedding gift. They moved the house to the village of Cutchoque's village green.

Also in 1658, John Budd, as a member of the Southold Church, was fined fifteen pounds for letting Quakers assemble in his home. He said that "they were the honestest and most godly people that were now in the world" and were "worse treated in New Haven Colony than elsewhere." But John Budd was an independent sort of man. For, according to <u>Early Long Island Wills, Suffolk Co. 1691-1703</u>, the next year, John Budd sold a lot and house to a Quaker, causing a great deal of upheaval in the community.

According to <u>The Fathers of New England</u>, Quakers were seen as "ranter, heretics." In Boston their books were burned because they were "corrupt, heretical and blasphemous." Also in Boston, in the beginning they were "sent back to Barbados whence they cam." Later, Quakers were mutilated and, finally, in October, 1658, four were hanged.

From 1664 through 1668, a "Jon Budd" was proprietor and representative or judge of the Township of Rye in Fairfield Co., Connecticut. Perhaps this was the same John Budd. Or perhaps it was his son, John, who bought his father's house on Tucker's

Lane when his father died in 1678. Half of the house was sold to the blacksmith, Jeremiah Vail, Jr. on April 28, 1679. The other half of the house was sold to either John Cory or John Hallock. Eventually the house became a tavern.

John Budd III was born in 1620, the year Plymouth, Massachusetts was founded. He was christened in the same church in Stepney, England as his father. He was first listed as being in "Yennycock" (Southold) in 1644 and was admitted as a freeman in 1645.

He may have married Mary Horton, daughter of Southold's baker, Barnabas Horton. Mary Horton would have more likely been the wife of John Budd IV who supposedly married Molly Horton, or to have been the second wife of John III. According to Southold's Town Records of 1658, "John Budds sonne John borne 14th Januarie". Other children of John III included Joseph, Ann, Hannah, and Marie. There was possibly another son, Jonathan, born in Rye, Connecticut.

In charge of the town forces in 1661, John III became known as Lt. John Budd. Occasionally he was listed also as a captain since he commanded a vessel.

A John Budd was listed as a representative for Greenwich (1664), for the United Colony of Connecticut (1666), and for Milford (1677). The following was taken from The Southold Town Records -

"Obteined of Mr. John Budd by was of exchange fifteen acres of land, lying on ye Wester' side of Jonathan Hortons North Sea lott, bounded by ye highway on ye West.
Entre pr Benj: Yongs, Rer 1682"
"Purchased of Mr. Budd one acre of meadow lying at South Harbour, bounded by Isaac Overton West and mr. John Bud East.
Entd   pr Benj: Yo. Rdr."

John Budd's will was listed in New York Calendar of Wills #47 (B2). "Only the last part of this will is extant, opting neighbors John Tuthil and Isaac Arnold, as executor. The will is approved in court of Ayer and Terminer for Suffolk c., N.Y. November 11, 1684." The will gave his daughter Mary Budd Youngs half of the lands and meadows belonging to him in the "Ackabork" division of Southold. Through his wife Mary, Christopher Youngs inherited from his father-in-law 10 cattle, 10 sheep, 1 horse, 1 mare, 2 swine, 5 pounds 10 shillings, and 2 pence. Another 23 pounds, 1 shilling, and 5 pence were assigned to pay off John III's debts.

According to Southold Town Records of 1654, Marie the daughter of John Budd was "borne in Septbr 1654." She married Christopher Youngs circa 1675. After her husband's death, Marie gave the land she had inherited from her father to her sons. She died sometime after 1723/24.

Chapter 4

Con(c)kling Family

Unknown
    Children
        Ananias (see below)
        John - b.c. 1600
            m. Elizabeth Allseabrook; January 24,
            1624/25; St. Peter's Church, Nottingham, England
            d.c. 1684
            Children
                John - b. 1630; Nottinghamshire, England
                    m. Sarah Solomon; December 2, 1653;
                    Southold, Long Island
                    d. April 6, 1694; Southold, Long Island
                    Children
                        John - b.c. 1650; Southold, Long
                            Island
                            m. Sarah, dau of Barnabas
                            Horton; 1675; Southold, Long
                            Island
                            Children
                                Joseph (Lt.) - b.c. 1686
                                    m. Lydia
                                    d. January 27,
                                    1742/43
                              Thomas - b.c. 1694/5
                                    m. Rachel (1704-
                                    1750)
                                    d. March 4, 1782
                            Mary - d. November 2,
                                1688
                          Elizabeth
                          Sarah
                          Rachel
                          John
                          Henry
                Timothy - 1640; Salem, Massachusetts
                    m. Sarah Scudder
                    d. 1720

Ananias
    b.c. 1600
    m. Mary Launders/Landers; February 23, 1630/1; St. Peter's
    Church, Nottingham, England
    d.c. 1657; Easthampton, Long Island
    Children
        Jeremiah (see below)
        Lewis - bapt. April 30, 1643
        Elizabeth - b. March 18, 1649
        Jacob

Jeremiah
    b.c. 1634
    m. Mary (1638-1689), dau of Lion Gardiner
    d. 1712
    Children
        Mary - m. Thomas (d. 1727 or 1731), son of William and
            Sarah Mulford of Easthampton, Long Island
            d. after 1727
            Children
                Thomas   William

Rachel   Ezekiel
Abiah   Lawsons
David   Jeremiah

Chapter 5

Folger Family

John
    m. Elizabeth; Diss, Norfolk Co., England
    Children
        John (see below)

John Jr.
    b. 1594; Diss, Norfolk Co., England
    m. Merebah (d. 1664; Martha's Vineyard, Massachusetts), dau
    of John Gibbs (d. 1609) of Frenze Hall, Norfolk Co. England
    Children
        Mary (see below)
        Peter - b. 1617; Diss, Norfolk Co., England
            m. Mary Morell (d. 1704)
            Children
                Eleazer - b.c. 1648
                    m. Sarah Gardner
                John - b.c. 1659
                Abiah - b. August 15, 1667; Nantucket,
                    Massachusetts
                    m. Josiah Franklin; November 29, 1689
                    d. 1749
                    Children
                        Peter - b. November 22, 1692
                            m. Mary
                            d. July 1, 1766
                        Mary - b. September 26, 1694
                            m. Robert Holmes
                        James - b. February 4, 1696
                            m. Anne
                            d. February, 1735
                        Sarah - b. January 9, 1699
                            m. Joseph Davenport
                            d. May 23, 1731
                        John - b. December 7, 1699
                            m. Gooch
                            d. 1759
                      Ebenezer - September 20, 1701
                            d. Young
                      Thomas - b. December 7, 1703
                            d. Young
                      Benjamin - b. January 6, 1706
                            m. Deborah Reed; September 1,
                          1730
                          d. April 17, 1790
                      Lydia - b. August 8, 1708
                          m. Robert Scott, 1731
                      Jane - b. March 27, 1712
                          m. Edward Macon; July 27,
                          1727
                          d. 1795
                Joanna - m. John, son of Thomas and Johanna
                  Coleman
                Bethia - m. John, son of Robert and Joanna
                  Barnhill or Barnard
                Patience - m1. Ebenezer Harker
                  m2. James Gardner of Salem
              Experience - m. John Swain, Jr.
               Dorcas
               Bathshua

Mary
       b. after 1617
       m1. Peter Paine (b. March 14, 1616; Wentrom, Suffolk Co.,
       England; d. 1658; Southold, Long Island); New England
       m2. Jeremiah Vail; May 24, 1660
       d. by 1685
       Children
              John - b. 1663; Southold, Long Island
                     m. Grace Brockett, c. 1684
                     d. August 18, 1737; Southold, Long Island
              David or Daniel - b. 1665; Southold, Long Island
              Mary - b. 1667; Southold, Long Island
                     d. September 22, 1689; Southold, Long Island

       John Folger (Foulgier, Ffoulger), Jr. was born in 1594 in
Diss, Norwich, Norfolk Co., England to John and Elizabeth
Folger. Diss, a market town on the Waveney River, was actually
19 miles southwest of Norwich. Folger's great-grandson,
Benjamin Franklin, once said he believed John was the son of
Flemish refugees who migrated to England in the time of
Elizabeth I.

       That corresponds with history for, according to
Tourtellot's Benjamin Franklin: The Shaping of Genius, in the
later part of the 16th century, the Flemish were increasingly
dissatisfied with the theology forced on Flanders and Walloon by
Charles V's Holy Roman Empire. After Philip II, King of Spain,
succeeded Charles V, the Council of Blood was established in
1567 to end all Protestant opposition to the Roman Church. The
Flemish and Walloons fled and migrated to Protestant England.

       They were an industrious, artistic people whose primary
trade was cloth weaving. Many of the refugees settled in
Norwich which had been the weaving center of England since the
late 1300's. Norwich was an ancient city dating back before 900
A.D. At the Norman Conquest in 1066 A.D., Norwich was one of
England's largest cities with a population of 5500.

       According to Tourtellot, many Flemish had settled in the
Norwich area earlier. They had migrated to England after King
Edward III had married Philippa, daughter of William, Count of
Holland and Flanders. The area was rich with Flemish master
weavers. Tourtellot emphasized that in 1582, 3300 Netherlanders
and 1400 of their English born children were living in Norwich,
totaling over one-fourth of the city's population.

       And it was in Frenze Hall, Norfolk County where John's
future wife, Merebah or Meribel, was born to John and, possibly,
Alice Gibbs sometime after 1599. According to Directory of the
Ancestral Heads of New England Families, Gibbs was a surname
from "Gib", a nickname of Gilbert. The Gibbs family was a well
established family in Norfolk. In Calendar of Patent Rolls
1570-71, a John Gibbes was listed as alderman of Norwich in
Norfolk and, while alderman, was appointed to the commission for
sewers. On January 20, 1686/87, a Lady Gibbe was listed as a
resident of Norfolk. In Calendar of the Freemen of Norwich from
1317-1603, several Gibbes and Gibbys were listed, but no John.

       In 1615, John Folger and Merebah Gibbs were married in
Frenze Hall, two miles from Diss. According to Papers of
Benjamin Franklin, their son Peter was born in 1617 in Diss,
Norfolk Co. Their daughter was born later. In Franklin, David
Freeman Hawke described Folger family members as having large;

"square, homely" faces, heavy chests and shoulders and hazel eyes.

Widespread government controls and taxes on the cloth industry, a renewed war in the Netherlands disturbing the market there coupled with high unemployment and a depression in the cloth making centers developed in the 1620's. Netherlands and Spain prohibited import of English woolens, according to This New Man, The American. In 1629, partly because of bad harvests, widespread riots took place in southeastern among the unemployed weavers.

And when Queen Elizabeth I died, she was succeeded by James I who, according to Tourtellot, "denounced the non-conforming Protestants when he met with his first parliament in 1603". With the succession of Charles I, the problem was enhanced. Civil War was closer to a reality and many Flemish Protestants fled, some back to Holland, more to the New World.

Among them was John Folger and his family. He left Norwich because he refused to "put up with repression as his father before had refused to do in Flanders." Tourtellot went on to write "The very fact that the Folgers were a refugee family in Norwich made them both less inclined to stay there in the face of repression (England wasn't really home to them...) and less tolerant of the oppressiveness which, having been unwilling to put up with it in their homeland, they were not likely to accept it passively in an adopted land."

John's wife, Merebah Gibbs, was from a family who had rebelled against tyranny as far back as the 1230's. Since that time, periodic trouble had arisen between the wealthy monasteries of Norwich and the poor people in the area. A major Saxon town, Norwich boasted more than 30 medieval cathedrals and a Norman cathedral. There had been a bloody riot against the cathedral monks in 1272. In 1381 was the Peasants' Riot. In 1540, a rebel army of 20,000 Norwich farmers were defeated by the Earl of Warwick and their rebel leader was hung in Norwich Castle. By 1549, 3,000 of those Norwich rebels had died resisting enclosure of lands.

So in 1635, John and Peter Folger were listed as passengers on the "Abigail", landing in Boston on October 6. Merebah and Mary were not listed. Merebah and Mary may have followed on a different ship or, being women, may have been considered unimportant and left off of the "Abigail" passenger list. Alexander Starbuck, in History of Nantucket, stated that John Folger emigrated to America as a widower. However, since there was proof of their marriage in Diss, England, and since Merebah was buried next to John on Martha's Vineyard, it was highly unlikely. More likely they emigrated on separate ships, perhaps with the males of the family going ahead to prepare the way.

According to the July, 1862 "New England Historical and Genealogical Register" (NEHGR), on the "Abigail" with John and Peter was Hugh Peters, an English Puritan clergyman who later became the minister of the first church of Salem, Massachusetts. In 1641, Peters became an agent for the colony in England where he later filled important offices under Cromwell. At the Restoration, Peters was imprisoned in the Tower of London. He was doomed before his trial ever began and was convicted on October 13, 1660, as an accomplice to the execution of Charles I. Peters was hanged and quartered at Charing Cross, London.

John Winthrop, Jr. and Sir Henry Vane, a gifted lawyer, were also aboard the "Abigail" on John Folger's voyage. John Winthrop, Jr., eldest son of Governor Winthrop of Massachusetts, would become noted for the founding of Ipswich and New London and as a Governor of Connecticut. He was also acclaimed for his scientific accomplishments and has been called the "first American scientist".

The Boston of 1635 was only five years old when the passengers of the "Abigail" arrived. It had one church, no schools and no commerce.

In 1638, John Folger was proposed for property at Dedham, "a rude frontier community concentrated in a row of tiny cottages... with thatched roofs and no window glass," according to Tourtellot. The Folgers soon left and moved to the prosperous town of Watertown, three miles from Boston. But in 1642, John left a large house on six acres in Watertown to help settle Martha's Vineyard.

At Martha's Vineyard, John Folger owned a house; upland commonage and meadowland. John died in 1662 on Martha's Vineyard. His wife Merebah died in 1664 and was buried beside her husband on Tower Hill, Great Harbor, Martha's Vineyard, Massachusetts. The sale of Merebah's estate was dated October 18, 1664 and was handled by her son Peter. Thomas Mayhew purchased the estate.

In the NEHGR's "The Folger Family", by William Coleman Folger, Peter may have preceded his parents to Martha's Vineyard, going there with Thomas Mayhew, Jr. in 1641 or 1642. According to William Coleman Folger, Peter was a surveyor and taught Indians on the island. He married Mary Morrell, a former bonded servant of Rev. Hugh Peters. Peter bought her for 20 pounds, which he claimed was the best buy he ever made. Peter died on Nantucket Island in 1690. Mary died in 1704.

Peter and Mary would become the grandparents of Benjamin Franklin through their daughter Abiah. Hawke reported Franklin frequently recalled how much he owed to his mother's judgement and common sense. In The Private Franklin by Lopez and Herbert, the Folgers were described as "among the earliest settlers of Nantucket and (Franklin) remembered with obvious satisfaction the words spoken by his Quaker grandfather, Peter Folger, with 'decent plainness and manly freedom' in favor of liberty and conscience". Peter had defended liberty of conscience for Quakers and Anabaptists against intolerance. Franklin called his Folger relatives "wonderfully shy". He described them as plain spoken and often told the story of inviting two of his Folger relations to dinner. As Franklin wrote later, "Their answer was, that they would, if they could not do better."

Little was known about the early life of John and Merebah Folger's daughter, Mary. She was married first to Peter Paine who had been born in Suffolk County, England, on March 14, 1616. They lived in Southold, Long Island. His will was proven in 1658.

On May 24, 1660, Mary Folger Paine married second Jeremiah Vail, a widower who had recently moved to Southold, Long Island. Jeremiah was a blacksmith and, after his marriage to Mary, they lived on Peter Paine's old lot.

In 1663, Mary's son John Vail was born. He was followed by David/Daniel in 1665 and Mary in 1667. However, by July 18, 1685, Jeremiah had married for a third time and there was no more record of Mary Folger Paine Vail.

Chapter 6

Gardiner Family

Lion
     b. 1599
     m. Mary (d. 1665), dau of Derike Willemson of Worden,
     Holland
     d. 1663; Gardiner's Island, New York
     Children
          David (see below)
          Mary - b. August 30, 1638; Saybrook, Connecticut
               m. Jeremiah Conkling of Easthampton
               d. November 2, 1689
               Children
                    Mary - m. Thomas (d. 1727 or 1731), son of
                         William and Sarah Mulford of
                         Easthampton, Long Island
                         d. after 1727
                         Children
                              Thomas   Rachel
                              William   Ezekeel
                              Lawsons   Jeremiah
                              Abiah   David
          Elizabeth - b. September 14, 1641; Isle of Wright
               m. Arthur Howell of Southampton, Long Island
               d. 1664
               Children
                    Elizabeth

David
     b. April 29, 1636; Saybrook, Connecticut
     m. Mary Leringmore; June 4, 1657; St. Margaret,
     Westminister, England
     d. July 10, 1689; Hartford, Connecticut
     Children
          John - b. April 19, 1661
               m1. Mary King (d. July 4, 1707)
               m2. Sarah Cort (d. July 3, 1711)
               m3. Elizabeth (b.c. 1683, d. May 15, 1747)
               d. June 25, 1738; Groton, Connecticut
               Children
                    David   Mary   John
                    Samuel   Elizabeth   Joseph
                    Jonathan   Sarah   Hannah
                    Abigail
          Lion - d. September 23, 1723
               Children
                    Lion - d. 1781
                         Children
                              John
                              Lion
                              Jeremiah
                    Giles
          Elizabeth - m. James Parshall; 1678; Easthampton, Long
               Island
          David

     While Lion (Lyon, Lionel) Gardiner was not actually an
inhabitant of Southold, he was a powerful, moving force in the
settlement of eastern Long Island. His importance to the
Southold area dictates that he be included in this treatise.

The family name seemed to originate with the Norman word for "gardener", which was "gardinier". As might be expected, the Gardiner name was found among early peasant farmers. This particular family was thought to have originated in Scotland, although Thompson, in <u>History of Long Island</u>, placed Lyon as being English. Banks' <u>Topographical Dictionary</u> listed Gardiner as originating in Stepney, England, the same place as John Budd. However, as a suburb of London, Stepney could have been a stopping point between Holland and the New World.

Thompson described Gardiner as having a "bold and adventurous spirit, who, seeking fame or sympathizing with the oppressed" decided to work for the Dutch against Spain. To that end, he became master of fortifications for the Prince of Orange.

In Holland, Lion met and married a Dutch girl named Mary, daughter of Derike Willemson of Worden, Holland. Mary Powell Bunker, in <u>Long Island Genealogies</u>, quoted from Lion's Bible that Mary's mother was a Hackin and that her mother's sister married Wouter Leonardson.

While in Holland, Lion's expertise as an engineer came to the attention of English Puritans who had taken refuge there. Realizing they could use Lion's expertise, the Puritans decided to enlist his aid. Rev. Hugh Peters, who would later travel to the New World with the Folger family, hired Lion to build a strong fort at the mouth of the Connecticut River for Peter's step-son, John Winthrop, Jr. The agreement called for Lion to remain there for four years and to have 300 men under his command.

According to Thompson, Lion and Mary left Worden on July 10, 1635. After a short stay in London, they departed for the New World. The log was dated "11 Aug ti 1635. In the Balcheler de Lo. Master Tho. Webbors New England, Lyon Gardner 36 yers & his wife Mary 34 yers & Elisa. Colet 23 yers their maid servant & Wm Jope 40 yers who are to passe to New England have brought Cert. of their Conformity." According to both Savage and Thompson, the Gardiners were accompanied by eleven men. They arrived in Boston on November 28, 1635, before continuing on to complete fortifications at Fort Hill. Then they went to Salem to check fortifications there. But Lion reported Salem was in "more danger of starving then any foreign potent enemy".

In March, 1636, Lion and Mary went to Saybrook. The fort was named for Lord Say and Lord Brook, the patentees. Gardiner was to be the principal planter there. But when the Gardiners arrived Lion discovered promises that had been made to him had been broken. Thompson wrote that "he was furnished with barely men enough to garrison the fort" (see Appendix II).

While the Gardiners were are Saybrook, John Endicott and his troops; including Captain John Underhill, later of Southold; made repeated attacks on the Pequot Indians. After killing some Indians and burning crops and wigwams, Endicott's troops would be reinforced at Saybrook before going off again. Gardiner warned Endicott "you come hither to raise these wasps about my ears, and then you will take wigs and flee away". According to Rothbard in <u>Conceived in Liberty</u>, the Pequots were bitter and attacked Saybrook Fort. Thompson wrote that Gardiner was severely wounded. And, according to Bodge's <u>Soldiers in King Philip's War</u>, "The Saybrook garrison were (sic) in a state of siege for many months; and whenever they ventured from the fort, were followed by the savages, with intent to lure them into ambush". Bodge cited several incidents of capture, torture and death in the Saybrook area. In April, 1637, Indians attacked Wethersfield residents traveling near the fort. Six men and three women were killed and two girls were captured. Through his connections, Gardiner was able to obtain the girls' release.

Two of the Gardiners' children were born at Saybrook. Their son David was born April 29, 1636, and their daughter Mary was born on August 30, 1638.

James Farrett, a Scot, arrived in America in 1640, just as Lion's Saybrook contract was coming to an end. Farrett, as agent of the Earl of Stirling, was empowered to sell the Earl's charter to Monchonock Island to Gardiner, and Southampton and other areas of Long Island to others. Farrett's final sale, made shortly before his death, was the area which would become Southold.

Gardiner renamed his island the Isle of Wright, built a farm and moved his family. The island eventually became known as Gardiner's Island. According to Bunker, the Gardiner's Island settlement was the first English settlement in New York State and his daughter Elizabeth, born September 14, 1641, was the first English child born there. In the years to follow, Lion would hire Jeremiah Vail to work for him before Vail finally settled in Southold.

When Easthampton was settled on the adjacent shore, Lion, while maintaining control of Isle of Wright, moved his family to the new settlement and became one of the proprietors. The primary move was made in 1653, although Lion's son stayed behind to manage the island. Gardiner bought a home lot and Thomas James, Easthampton's first mill owner, paid 500 pounds for some other land in 1659. Records at Easthampton chronicled a ruling that half of all dead whales cast on the nearby shore would be given to Thomas James and Lion Gardiner.

Lion Gardiner died in 1663, leaving his entire estate to his wife (see Appendix II). When she died two years later, Mary willed the island to her son David. The land in Easthampton went to her daughter Mary and to her granddaughter Elizabeth by her deceased daughter, Elizabeth Gardiner Howell.

According to Thompson, in History of Long Island, Elizabeth Gardiner had been born on September 14, 1641, married Arthur Howell; had a daughter named Elizabeth; and died in February, 1657. Although much of Thompson's information was correct, this information indicated that by age 15 1/2, Elizabeth had married, had a child, and had died.

Lion's son David was the first white child born in Connecticut. Various sources agreed that David married a widow named Mary from St. Margarets, Westminster, England while he was in England being educated. While Leringmore has been the most accepted last name for his wife, Lungman and Herringham have also been suggested.

David was proprietor of Gardiner's Island for 23 years. Thompson implied that Lion had financial problems brought on by David's youthful extravagance. David died suddenly on a business trip to Hartford, Connecticut on July 10, 1689 at age 54.

According to his tombstone, he was "Well, sick, dead in one hours space."

John Gardiner, son of David and grandson of Lion, was the Lord of the Manor of Gardiner's Island when the Earl of Bellomont contacted him about Captain Kidd's treasure. According NEGHR's January, 1852 article concerning Captain Kidd, the Earl had heard "Kidds men had offered 30 pounds for a sloop to carry him to Gardiner's Island" the day Kidd was apprehended. The Earl ordered Gardiner to deliver "whatever Kidd had left with him." Gardiner delivered a treasure of gold, silver and jewels valued at 4500 pounds."

According to John Gardiner's account, given on July 17, 1699; in late June, Gardiner saw an armed sloop just off his island. Two days later, Gardiner went aboard to inquire why the boat was there. Captain Kidd answered he was going to Lord Bellomont and asked Gardiner to "keep 2 negro boys and 1 negro girl" until he returned. Gardiner agreed. Ten hours later, Kidd sent two bales and a negro boy ashore. The next morning, Kidd asked Gardiner to bring him six sheep for his voyage. Gardiner complied. Then Kidd requested a barrel of cider. While Gardiner's men went for the cider, Kidd presented Gardiner with some damaged "Muslin and Bengal". As he left, Kidd fired four guns. Three days later, Gardiner was sent for again. He wanted Gardiner to keep "a bundle of quilts, 4 bales of goods and a box of gold intended for Bellomont". Later Kidd's men delivered silver and gold and gold dust for Gardiner to keep. Gardiner claimed he "knew nothing of Kidd's being proclaimed a Pirate, and if he had, he durst not have acted otherwise, than he has done, having no force to oppose, and that he hath formerly been threatened to be killed by Privateers if he should carry unkindly to them." At the time, the entire inventory of Kidd's goods in Gardiner's possession was valued at $20,000.

In years to follow, pirates, buccaneers and regular people visited Gardiner's Island in search of more of Kidd's treasure. No more of the treasure has been found.

John Gardiner died in 1738. He was injured after being thrown from a horse and died 6 days later in Groton, Connecticut.

Gardiner descendants were numerous and included Captain Abraham Gardiner and Dr. Nathaniel Gardiner (1759-1801), an American Revolution surgeon, legislative representatives and shipping merchant. They were the sons of Abraham Gardiner (c.1720-1782) and his wife Mary.

Interestingly, only one slave appears to have been buried in the family cemetery, one named Peggy. She must have been especially cherished by Abraham Gardiner and his family because they erected a monument to her in the cemetery.

Chapter 7

Hallock Family

Peter
    b. England
    m. Mrs. Howell, England
    Children
        William

William
    m. Margaret
    d. 1684, 1688 or 1689
    Children
        John (see below)
        Peter - d. 1756
            Children
                Peter (Major) - d. 1791
                Noah - b. 1696
                    m. Bethia, dau of Josiah Young;
                    November, 1721
                    d. 1773; Blue Point, Long Island
                    Children
                        Noah - b. 1728
                        Josiah - b. 1732
                        William
        Elizabeth - m1. Harried
                    m2 - Richard Howell, 1675
        Abigail - Caleb Horton; December 23, 1665; Long Island
        Thomas
        Mary
        Martha
        Sarah

John
    m. Abigail (d. January 23, 1737; Westbury), dau of John
    Sweezey; 1679; Southold, Long Island
    d. May 25, 1737; Westbury
    Children
        John Jr. - b. 1680
            m. Hannah, by 1701
            r. Setauket, Long Island
            Children
                John III - b. 1701
                    m. Martha Quimby of Mamaroneck, Long
                    Island; 1737
                    d. 1757
                Sarah - b. 1702
                    m. Caleb Hunt, 1727
                Abigail - b. 1705
                    m. Thomas, son of Thomas and Mary
                    Willets Powell; 1707
                Hannah - b. 1707
                    m. Saterlys?
                Catherine - b. 1712
                    m. Moses, son of Thomas and Mary
                    Willets Powell; 1732
                Edward - b. 171
                    m. Phebe, dau of John and Dorcas Quimby
                    Clapp
                    d. 1810
                Phebe - b. 1720
                    m. Abraham, son of Abraham Underhill;

```
                     1746
            Clement - b. 1723
                     m. Caleb, son of Caleb and Sarah
                     Powell; 1752
            Samuel - b. 1725
                     m. 1754
            Almy b. 1727
                     m. Jacob, son of Abraham Underhill;
                     1747
      Margaret - b. 1682
            m. John (d. 1738), son of Thomas Powell; October,
            1704
      Abigail - b. 1688
            d. unmarried
      Benjamin - m. Sarah
      Catherine - m. Thomas, son of Thomas (1650-1710) and
            Dinah Townsend Willets; 1706
      Sarah - m. Richard, son of Thomas (1650-1710) and
            Dinah Townsend Willets
      Mary - m. Amos, son of Thomas (1650-1710) and Dinah
            Townsend Willets; 1713
      Climent - m. Isaac ( 1736), son of Thomas (1650-1710)
            and Dinah Townsend Willets; 1716
      Peter - m. Abigail, dau of Thomas and Mary Willets
            Powell
      William
```

Peter Hallock (Halliock or Holliock) was one of the thirteen original settlers who landed in the Southold area. He was the first to step ashore at an area afterwards called Hallock's Neck.

According to French's Historical and Statistical Gazetteer of New York, Hallock first settled on land ten miles west of Southold, Long Island, that he purchased from the Indians in 1641. His original homestead, two miles west of present Mattituck, reached from Long Island Sound to the Peconic Bay, three miles away.

Hallock had traveled to the New World alone. Once he was settled, he returned to England to get his wife, the former Mrs. Howell, and children. French stated that while Hallock was in England, John Tuthill; John Youngs, Jr.; John King; and Israel, Richard and Samuel Brown moved onto his land and took possession.

In Mary Powell Bunker's version in Long Island Genealogies, when Hallock returned to England for his family, his wife refused to return with him to the New World until he agreed to give her two daughters by a former marriage large tracts of land. After two to three years of "negotiating", they finally emigrated, only to find Hallock's land in the possession of another party. Bunker wrote that the Indians had resold the land. Peter finally settled on Mattituck land, where his descendants lived for hundreds of years.

Bunker reported that in 1654, Peter's son William "was in possession of a large Property" in Southold and "was quite a man of business in the town". William died in 1684, 1688 or 1689, depending upon the source; leaving his wife Margaret as executrix.

An article entitled "Early New Yorkers and Their Ages" in the "National Genealogical Society Quarterly" listed a William "Hallet", born in Dorsetshire, England, as living in Flushing at age forty on November 8, 1656. William Hallet might have been the William Hallock of this genealogy.

His son John's marriage to Abigail Sweezy caused a split in the Hallock family. William was a staunch member of the Church of England, while Abigail's family were Salem Quakers. According to Bunker, when John married Abigail, William disinherited his son. The young couple moved to Westbury where John eventually died on May 25, 1737, four months after Abigail's death.

The Benjamin Hallock who died in 1765 in Southold, Long Island may have been the son of John and Abigail. However, according to his October 22, 1765 will, that Benjamin named his brother Zerubbabel as administrator of his estate. Zerubbabel has not appeared as a child of John and Abigail.

According to the DAR lineage books, a William Hallock, who was possibly the son of Noah 5 (Peter 4, Peter 3, William 2, Peter 1), "responded to the Bennington Alarm under Captain Christopher Banister" as a minuteman in 1777. He also skippered a sailing vessel against the British. That William was born in Brookhaven, Long Island in 1730, married Alice Homan and died in Goshen, Massachusetts.

Also see Brockett Family

Chapter 8

Horton Family

Barnabas
    b. July 13, 1600; Mowsley, Leicestershire, England
    m1. Anne Smith; Northamptonshire, England
    m2. Mary Landon (Langton) by 1640
    d. July 13, 1680; Southold, Long Island
    Children by Anne
        Joseph - b. 1625; Mowsley, Leicestershire, England
            m. Jane, dau of John Budd; Southold, Long Island
        Benjamin - b. 1627; Mowsley, Leicestershire, England
            m. Anna, dau of John Budd; c. 1661; Southold,
            LongIsland
            d. November 3, 1690; Rye, New York
    Children by Mary
        Caleb - b. 1640; Southold, Long Island
            m. Abigail, dau of William Hallock; December 23,
            1665; Southold, Long Island
            d. October 3, 1702; Cutchoque, Long Island
            Children
                Barnabas - b. September 23, 1666; Southold,
                    Long Island
                    m. Sarah, dau of Barnabas Wines;
                    Southold, Long Island
                    d. December, 1696
                    Children
                        Caleb - b. December 22, 1687
                          m. Phebe Terry; December,
                          1709
                          d. August 6, 1772; Roxbury,
                          New Jersey
                        Bethia - b.c. 1688
                          m. Thomas Reeve
                          d. February 4, 1715;
                          Southold, Long Island
                      Penelope - b. February 4, 1690
                          m. Samuel "Swayze", c. 1709
                          d. December, 1746; Roxbury,
                          New Jersey
                  Barnabas
        Joshua - b. 1643; Southold, Long Island
            m. Mary Tuthill
        Capt. Jonathan - b.c. 1648; Southold, Long Island
            m. Bethia Wells
            d. February 27, 1707
        Hannah - b.c. 1651; Southold, Long Island
            m. Barnabas, son of Thomas Terrill; c. 1670;
            Southold, Long Island
            Children

Barnabas	Richard	Abigail
Nicholas	Catherine	Mary

        Sarah - b.c. 1653; Southold, Long Island
            m. John, son of John Conkling; 1675; Southold,
            Long Island
            Children

Sarah	Rachel	Mary
Joseph	John	Henry
Thomas	Elizabeth	

        Mary/Molly - b. 1655; Southold, Long Island
            m. John, son of John Budd; c. 1674
            d. aft 1680; Rye, New York

                    Children
                        John
                        Joseph
                        Jonathan
                        Others
            Mercy - b.c. 1660; Southold, Long Island
                m. Christopher Young, c. 1678
                Children
                        Nathaniel - b. 1683; Southold, Long Island
                        John - b. October 21, 1679; Southold, Long
                        Island
                        Abram - b. 1681; Southold, Long Island
            Abigail (adopted) - b.c. 1665; Southold, Long Island
                m. Charles, son of John Booth; c. 1690
                Children
                        Charles - b. 1691, Southold, Long Island
                            m. Mary (d. April 13, 1774)
                        Abigail - b. 1693; Southold, Long Island
                            m. Thomas Goldsmith
                        David - b. 1695; Southold, Long Island
                            m. 1717

        The name Horton came from the English word "horr" meaning
"ravine" or "a town in the ravine". Barnabas Horton may have
been from the small hamlet of Horton, Buckinghamshire, England;
fourteen miles from London and four miles from Leighton Buzzard.
However, more likely he was born on July 13, 1600 in Mowsley,
(Mousley) Leicestershire, England. An historically important
area, Leicestershire was the earldom of Simon de Montfort,
leader of the baron's revolt against Henry III which brought
about the first parliament. Leicester Castle, a Saxon
stronghold, was rebuilt by Normans in 1086. Cardinal Wolsey
died in the abbey there in 1530. Mowsley, however, eventually
disappeared from English maps.

        According to Hortons of Leicestershire by L.G.H. Horton
Smith, Henry de Horton of Horton, Northampton Co., first arrived
in Knaptoft, Leicester Co. between 1268 and 1277. From his son
Hugh's time on, the Horton family resided in Knaptoft and
Mowsley. While the Knoptoft branch migrated circa 1332, the
Mowsley branch remained. The Hortons were "a leading family in
Mowsley village throughout the Tudor period". Barnabas may have
been the great-grandson of Richard Horton of Mowsley, who was
born circa 1450; married Anne; and had William, Thomas and
Richard.

        In The Compendium of American Genealogy, Barnabas was
listed as the son of Joseph Horton. In Leicestershire Marriage
Licenses, 1570-1729, Barnabas' 1621 marriage to Anne Smith of
Stanyon was recorded in Book 2, fo. 24 and 25. Also listed in
Book 2 was the 1619 marriage of a Joseph Horton of Mowsely to
Elizabeth Bolesworth of North Kilworthe. Possibly Joseph was
Barnabas' brother. Joseph was also the name Barnabas chose for
his eldest son.

        According to Warren Hall's Pagans, Puritans, Patriots of
Yesterday's Southold, Barnabas Horton was "a big, strong, ruddy-
faced, genial man" who was a baker by trade, but could make a
living doing almost anything. The Hortons of America credited
him with "fine social qualities."

        In 1635, Anne Smith Horton and their two young children
emigrated with Barnabas on board the "Swallow" to settle in

                                35

Hampton, Massachusetts where Barnabas had a grant of land. Captain Jeremiah or Jeremy Horton was master and owner of the "Swallow" from 1635-1638.

On October 21, 1640, with a different wife, Barnabas was one of the organizers of the Congregational Church of the new town of Southold, Long Island.

As a leading citizen of Southold, he went on to serve as deputy of the General Court in New Haven during years between 1654 and 1664. He became a freeman of Connecticut Colony in 1662 and was one of the town's patentees, along with his son Joshua in 1676.

According to "The Hortons" in the October 15, 1953 "Long Island Traveler," Barnabas built the first frame home on eastern Long Island. In his book, Warren Hall wrote "Barnabas Horton and four of his sons had the most land and wealth - 1188 pounds worth - of the 82 taxpayers of Southold in 1675." Joseph had already left Southold, moving to Rye, New York in 1665. The house he had owned in present-day Cutchoque was purchased from him by his father for Joseph's brother Joshua. In 1661, while in Rye, Joseph served as lieutenant just prior to King Philip's War.

While Barnabas was a baker, son Joshua was a carpenter and son Jonathan was the first captain of the Suffolk Co. cavalry; agriculture was the main source of their wealth. A new crop, tobacco, had brought them high prices abroad giving them a lucrative business. The new industry also brought slaves to the area. In the late 1600's, there were 800 whites, 40 Indians and 41 blacks in Southold.

Barnabas Horton died in 1690. According to Hall's book, the large blue slate slab on his tomb was imported from Leicestershire, England. And, according to The Hortons in America, Barnabas wrote his own epitaph and had it carved into the stone before his death.

> To the partaker of this blessed life
> And you, dear children, all follow the Lord
> Hear and obey His public sacred word
> And in your houses call upon His name
> For oft I have advised you to the same:
> Then God will bless you with your children all
> And to this blessed place He will call
>
> Heb xi4 "He being dead, yet speaketh"

His son Caleb had Barnabas Horton, born at Catchogue, Long Island. That Barnabas married Sarah "Windes" (Wines). Many researchers have claimed he married Sarah Hines. However, Kinn Stryker-Rhodda, in "Sarah, Wife of Barnabas Horton (1666-1696) of Southold, Long Island," made a good case that his wife was actually Sarah "Windes" (Wines). Using the 1698 census, Barnabas "Windes" will and common names, Stryker-Rodda demonstrated that shortly after Barnabas Horton's death, his wife Sarah and daughter Penelope moved in with Sarah's sister Elizabeth and her husband Thomas Hunter. Their son Barnabas was living with his grandfather Caleb Horton. Daughter Bethia was living with her other grandfather, Barnabas Wines, who Stryker-Rhodda referred to as Barnabas "Windes". Son Caleb was living in Richard Terry's household.

In 1698, Eleazer Luce went to Southold from West Tisbury, Martha's Vineyard and, shortly after, married Sarah Wines Horton. They had their first child together circa 1700.

Chapter 9

Landon Family

George
    b. Herefordshire, England
    m1. by 1619, England
    m2. Hannah, wid of Edmund Haynes; 1648; Connecticut
    d. December 29, 1676; Wethersfield, Connecticut
    Children
        John (see below)
        Hannah - m. Nathaniel Pritchett
            Children
                Esther - m. John Hanset (Hanchett)
        Deliverance - m. Thomas Hanset (Hanchett)
        Esther - b. August 22, 1649
            m. John Hannum
        Daughter - m. _____ Corbee

John
    b. 1619; Herefordshire, England
    m2. Mary, wid of Thomas Gridley, dau of Robert Seymour;
    February 7, 1653
    d. 1683 or 1689
    Children
        Daniel (see below)
        David - b.c. 1650
            m. Martha
            d. 1725; New Bedford, New Hampshire
            Children
                David - b. September 20, 1685; Boston,
                    Massachusetts
                Samuel - b. 1686
                Jonathan - b. 1688
                Abigail - b. August 26, 1689
                    m. William Merchant; September 16, ??
                Elizabeth - b. May 15, 1692
                    m. Samuel Hood, 1731
                Benjamin - b. Dec, 1693
                    m. Rachel Gridley; April 28, 1719
                Joseph - b. November 22, 1696
                    m. Joanna Shote; April 27, 1719
                Mary - b. 1698
                Martha - b. 1701
                Sarah - b. 1704
        Samuel - bapt. February, 1653
            m. Elizabeth, wid of _____ Turner
            d. August 4, 1683
            Children
                John
                Samuel
        Joseph - bapt. 1660; Farmington, Connecticut
            d. April 21, 1715
            Children
                Sarah - bapt. June 6, 1697
                Joseph - bapt. June 6, 1697
                Samuel
                John
        James - m. Elizabeth
        Nathan - b. 1664
            m. Hannah Bishop (1671-1701); betw January 26,
            1692 and 1695
            d. March 9, 1718; Southold, Long Island

        Children
            Nathan - b. September 16, 1696; Southold,
                Long Island
                m. Prudence Osman; September 19, 1723
                d. September 28, 1750
            Elizabeth - b. by 1698; Southold, Long
                Island
                d. April 28, 1707/8
            James - d. young
            Samuel b. May 26, 1699; Southold, Long
                Island
                m1. Bethia Tuthill
                m2. Mary Youngs
                d. January 21, 1782
                Children
                    Henry - b. October 30, 1721-35
                        d. August 27, 1735
                    Hannah - b. November 2, 1724
                        m. _____ Brown
                    Nathan - b. 1734
                    Jared - b. 1740
                        m1. Martha, dau of Col.
                        Elijah Hutchinson; 1768;
                        Southold, Long Island
                        Children
                            Bethield/Bethia -
                                unmarried
                            Mary - m. William
                                Hubbard
                                of Guilford
                            Elijah
                    Jonathan - b. October 30, 1743;
                        Southold, Long Island
                        m. Isabella Gordon or Graham
                        d. 1815; Dutchess Co., New
                        York
                    David - b. October 30, 1743;
                        Southold, Long Island
                        d. September 14, 1796
                        Children
                            George
                    Samuel - d. young

Daniel
    b. 1650; Farmington, Connecticut
    m. Ann
    Children
        James (see below)
        Mercy - b. June 22, 1682; Bristol, Massachusetts
        Martha - b. February 4, 1683; Bristol, Massachusetts
        Elizabeth - b. September 24, 1686; Bristol,
            Massachusetts
        Mary
        Ann
        Lydia

James
    b. March 29, 1685; Bristol, Massachusetts
    m1. Mary Vail; May, 1707; Southold, Long Island
    m2. Mary, wid of Alexander Wilmont of Southampton, Long
    Island; June 12, 1723
    d. September 19, 1738; Litchfield, Connecticut
    Children

Mary - b. November 26; 1707; Southold, Long Island
    m. Rev. Abram Reeves (April 22, 1707-May 16,
    1798); October 16, 1732
    d. May 16, 1798; Southold, Long Island
Joseph - December 18, 1708
    m. Margaret
    d. Southold, Long Island
    Children
        Anne - d, April 16, 1741; Southold, Long
            Island
        Glennana - d. September 7, 1754; Southold,
            Long Island
        James - d. August 26, 1756; Southold, Long
            Island
        Nathan - d. young; Southold, Long Island
James - b. August 5, 1711
    m. Sarah Bishop (b. August 28, 1713)
    Children
        Asa - b. July 27, 1736
        Ezekiel - b. August 31, 1738
        Thomas - b. September 10, 1740
        Rachel - b. October 11, 1742
        Ambrose - b. September 9, 1744
            Children
                John R.
        Lois - b. July 11, 1746
        Luther - m. Mary Sheldon of Vermont
        Sarah
        James
        Samuel
        Nabby
        Nancy
Rachel - b. October 12, 1716; Southold, Long Island
    m. Samuel Moore (b. 1715; Southold, Long Island)
    d. Salisbury, Connecticut
    9 Children
David - b. July 5, 1718; Southold, Long Island
    m1. Mary, dau of Thomas Osborn; Easthampton, Long
    Island
    m2. Thankful Dickinson; Hatfield, Massachusetts
    Children
        Mary - b. November 22, 1739
            m. Archelus Bell
        David - b. October 13, 1741
            m. Chloe Buell
John - b. July 21, 1720; Southold, Long Island
    m. Katherine White (d. July 24, 1776); November
    2, 1741
    d. "Sugar Hill", Salisbury, Connecticut
    Children
        John - b. July, 1742
            m. Mary (Polly) Hanchett; December 25,
            1762
        James - b. September 24, 1744
        Mary - b. February 27, 1747
            m. Jacob Smith
        George - b. June 3, 1749
            m. Ruth Foster
        Orriente - b. 1751/2
            m. John Harris
        Katherine - b. May 4, 1754
            m. Asaph Beebe
        Elizabeth b. September 27, 1756

```
                    m. David Ives
              Rufus - b. February 4, 1759
                    m. Sarah Hunt
              Hannah - b. April 29, 1761
              David - b. July 4, 1763
        Lydia - b. 1722; Southold, Long Island
              m. Jonathan Buell (d. August 26, 1796)
              10 Children
        Nathan and/or William - b. April 15, 1727
              m. Sussex, New Jersey
              Children
                    Thomas        James
                    Nathaniel     Laban
        Ann
        Daniel - b. January 7, 1714; Southold, Long Island
              m2. Martha Youngs; May 22, 1736; Southold, Long
              Island
              d. July 11, 1790; Litchfield, Connecticut
              Children
                    Daniel - b. February 11, 1737
                          m. Chloe Smith
                          d. April, 1814
                    Abner - b. March 10, 1739
                          m. Eunice Gibb
                          d. 1795, Canada
                          Children
                                Mehitable  b. June 5, 1767
                                      m. David, son of Lt. Ephraim
                                      and Hannah Sanford Harrison
                    Molly - b. April 6, 1743
                          m. Sylvanus Bishop
                    John - b. May 14, 1747
                          m. Abigail Bissel
                    Seth - b. December 18, 1749
                          m1. Anna (1754-1800), dau of Zopher and
                          Elizabeth Wadham Beach
                          m2. Eunice (1751-1801), dau of Moses
                          and Rachel Goodwin Seymour
                          d. February 4, 1832; Litchfield,
                          Connecticut
                    Nathan - b. June 8, 1752
                          m. Sally Smith
                    Oliver - b. March 12, 1755; Litchfield,
                          Connecticut
                          m1. Aner Watkins (1754-1800); May 2,
                          1776
                          m2. Lois Loomis (May 27, 1761-July 20,
                          1825); September 13, 1809
                          d. 1820; Lansdowne, Canada
                          Children
                                Joseph    Benjamin  Oliver
                                Wm Henry  Simcoe    Erastus
                                Luther    Daniel    Jesse
                                Lois
                    Joseph - b. February 3, 1758; Litchfield,
                          Connecticut
                          d. August 24, 1775
```

    The present day Landon (Landin, Lauden, Lindon, Lindoll,
Lander, Langdon, Langston, Lankton) family was formed by the
uniting of two ancient French families. The Morins were from
old nobility originally from Maine, France (see Appendix III).
Several branches were formed: one was established in Normandy.

Meanwhile the towns of Loudun and Loudunois were detached from Poitou and given to the Comte d'Anjou by Guillaume, Duc of Aquitane. Loudun was the center for the provinces of Anjou, Louraine and Maine and a stronghold of French Protestants. Later Geoffroy the Bel, Comte d'Anjou, gave his town to Geoffroy, his second son, since his brother Henri had become King of England. These were the first Seigneurs de Loudun (Lords of Loudun).

The nobility from Maine and Loudun were united in 1298 when Geoffroy Morin, Seigneur du Tronchet au Maine, married Alix, the daughter of Richard, Seigneur de Loudun. Alix's first son inherited her father's title through her. However, the Morin de Loudun family was a divided one. While a few were Catholic, many were Protestant, even to the point of fighting and dying in the religious wars.

And that religious difference was the primary reason the family left France. In 1545, Francis I authorized the massacre of 3000 Protestants. Protestantism was formally banned in France in 1585 and the Catholic religion was practiced exclusively. Clergy were forced to leave the country and their parishioners had to choose between Catholicism and exile within six months. It was not until 1598 when the Edict of Nantes was signed that Protestants were supposedly given equal rights with Catholics. But in reality, under the edict, Protestants were only granted a limited freedom of worship.

When the family emigrated to England, the "Morin de" was dropped. Then, through the years, Loudun became Anglicized as "Landon".

Confusion abounds as to where the first American Landon was born. One possible site was Loudham Manor in Suffolk Co., England, near where Rev. John Young's was born. Another place frequently claimed was Hertforshire, England, a south midland county bounded by Greater London. As emigrants from France, it would be logical to move to an area near London.

The other possible place frequently given was Hereford in the west midlands of England bordering on the Welsh counties of Powys and Givent. That area was described by Sir William Addison in <u>Understanding English Place-Names</u> as reflecting "a way of life more akin to that of Wales then anyother part of England". He described the inhabitants as "country folks" with Welsh-sounding names.

The similarity of the two names - Herefordshire and Hertfordshire - was probably the cause for the confusion. One source of the confusion was a notation in a family Bible which gave "Hersford" as the place. Several Welsh homelands were cited in J.O. Landon's book. H.S. Landon wrote "A Mr. Landon, given name not known, was born in Wales, England in the year 1640". William Richard Cutler wrote "The name Landon is of Welsh origin."

But the source of their information could have been questionable, like Nathan Landon's cemetery monument. "A native of Wales" appeared on Nathan Landon's monument in the Southold, Long Island cemetery. However, the monument was erected a good deal after Nathan's death. The "March 9, 1718" and "A.E. 54 ys" on the stone were more modern ways of writing the information.

And one death date for his wife does not agree with her death date given elsewhere on the monument.

George left England for the same reasons his ancestors had left France - religious persecution. As with the Folgers, if the Landons would not put up with it in their own country, they certainly would not accept it in their adopted one. Between 1630 and 1640 persecution in England was at its height and the New England Colonies grew rapidly. In addition, new taxes were being imposed to pay for English wars and land was not plentiful.

George arrived in Boston in 1640. With him was his son John who had been born in England in 1619, the year of the first representative colonial assembly in America. George's wife and other children did not accompany them at that time, or, being females, were not listed.

George Landon was in Wethersfield, Connecticut in 1640 and in Springfield, Connecticut in 1646. Wethersfield, founded by John Oldham in 1634, was primarily an agricultural town. It had undergone a major set-back when, in 1637, the town had been attacked by Pequot Indians who killed many of the settlers. Springfield stood on major Indian trails and a major river, making it a center for beaver trade.

By 1648 George's first wife had died and, according to Genealogical Guide to the Early Settlers of America, on June 29th of that year, George married Hannah, the widow of Edmund Haynes. A daughter, Esther, was born on August 22, 1649.

Circa 1658, George moved to Northampton, Connecticut where he died in 1676. In addition to his children, George also mentioned his grandson Samuel in his will.

His son John Landon was not an original settler of Farmington, Connecticut; but he bought land there in 1650 and became an early proprietor and one of its leading citizens. According to Farmington Town Clerks by Mabel Hurlburt, He owned lots numbered 32, 37, 41 and 74A at one time.

His first wife is unknown, but at least one son, Daniel, and possibly more, were born to them. His first wife had died by 1653.

John became good friends with Thomas Gridley, a former soldier in the Pequot fight under Captain Mason. According to "English Home and Ancestry of Richard Seamer" (NEGHR) by George Seymour, Thomas had married Mary Seymour at Hartford, Connecticut on September 29, 1644.

When Thomas was dying, he asked his friend John Landon to administer his estate and care for his wife and his three children. Thomas' wife was Mary Seymour Gridley, sister of Richard Seymour (Semer, Seamer, Simmor, Seymore) of Hartford, Connecticut.

Some researchers have reported that Mary was Richard's daughter. Richard did have a daughter named Mary who, according to parish records in Sawbridgeworth, England, was baptized January 9, 1634/5. However, in those same records was "Mary, the daughter of Richard Semer was Buryed Aprill 3," 1635. That

Mary, had she lived, would have only been 9 or 10 years old when Mary Seymour married Thomas Gridley.

More likely, Mary Seymour Gridley and Richard Seymour, were the children of Robert and Elizabeth who married in Sawbridgeworth, Herts Co., England on November 14, 1603. Elizabeth was the daughter of John and Elizabeth (Bayford) Waller. Robert was the son of John (c. 1535 - 1605) Seymour of Sawbridgeworth, and his second wife Dyzory Porter.

John Landon did a good job taking care of Mary Seymour Gridley after Thomas' death, for, according to <u>Genealogical Guide to the Early Settlers of America</u>, on February 7, 1653, they were married in Farmington, Connecticut. On his wedding day, John joined the church where he would later become deacon. He was only 34 years old when he started his second family.

Twelve to fifteen children were born to John Landon by either his first wife or Mary. Among them were John, Joseph, David, James and Nathan, in addition to Daniel. There were at least two additional children, Elizabeth and Samuel, but their paternity - Thomas Gridley or John Landon - remained unclear.

In <u>"First Settler" Oliver Landon of Lansdowne</u>, Truman Landon stated "John Langton" was listed as having paid his debts to the estate of Capt. Robert Button in 1652. Many of the Suffolk Co. wills had long lists of people indebted to an estate. Many of these were captains' estates and appeared to be debts for passage to the New World. Peter Paine of Southold, Long Island also paid a debt to Capt. Button in 1652.

John died in 1689, the year William and Mary recognized the old charters of the English Colonies.

His son David fought under Capt. Mosley in King Philip's War and was paid 2 pounds 14 shillings 10 pence on July 24, 1676. Previously he had served under Capt. James Oliver at the garrison at Mendon. He received a land grant in New Bedford, New Hampshire.

John's son James served with his brother David for part of the time during the war. He eventually owned land in Swansey, Lynn and elsewhere.

John's son Nathan married Hannah Bishop of Guilford, Connecticut before removing to Southold, Long Island. A Mary Landon (Langton) had married Barnabas Horton before he settled in Southold in 1640. Could Nathan have gone to Southold because relatives were already living there? According to the Southold records, Nathan took a "house lott adjoining to John Paine on the East and James Patty on the West" on November 20, 1668. However, since Nathan was born in 1664, the information is questionable. In 1711 Nathan was mentioned as purchaser of 16 acres from Jemima Paine.

Nathan and Hannah had three sons. James died young. Nathan II inherited the homestead and other lands from his father, but gave the homestead to his brother Samuel.

According to the DAR lineage books, his son Jonathan (Samuel 4, Nathan 3, John 2, George 1) was born in Southold in 1743. He married Isabella Graham and served under Col. Morris Graham, his brother-in-law, in the Rhinebeck Military Regiment during the Revolutionary War. During the war Jonathan was also a delegate to the Provincial Congress in 1775 and a member of the Senate from 1777 to 1779. In addition, he worked on fortifying Albany and helped build barracks and guard cannons at Kingsbridge. Jonathan died in Dutchess Co., New York in 1815.

Jonathan's great-uncle (John Landon's son) Daniel was harder to trace. He was born in 1650 in Farmington, Connecticut. During King Philip's War he was a scout under Col. Scott and was corporal defending the fort at Black Point on January 25, 1675/6. On June 24, 1676, he was paid 2 pounds 2 shillings for serving under Maj. Thomas Savage. On June 24, 1676, he was stationed with Moses Paine under Maj. Savage and Lt. Gillam (His son later married Mary Folger Paine). That same year, while still serving under Maj. Savage, Daniel was badly injured when his horse fell on ice, was dismissed from the service and received a soldier's land grant for Bristol. His petition for dismissal is in the State House Archives in Boston.

Of his children, Mercy was born in 1682, Martha in 1683, James in 1685 and Elizabeth in 1686. All were born in Bristol. On January 27, 1686/7, Daniel Landon sold 10 acres in Taunton, Bristol Co., Massachusetts to Nathaniel Paine. In 1689 Daniel Landon, along with his wife and 7 children appeared in the Bristol, Plymouth Colony Census, as did Joseph Landon and his wife.

Through the years, Landon genealogists have assumed the "Bristol" mentioned in Daniel's land grant and children's birth places was Bristol, Rhode Island. But most likely, Daniel lived in Bristol Co., Massachusetts, especially since the land grant was issued through Boston, Massachusetts and he sold land in Bristol Co., Massachusetts.

The confusion stemmed from a 1900 letter written to J.O. Landon, author of the most widely used and fairly accurate Landon genealogy, from the town clerk of Bristol, Rhode Island. The clerk, Herbert Bennett, wrote that the only Daniel Landon he found was in the "Records of Taunton, Mass." Since "Bristol" had been mentioned in a number of sources, and since the clerk of Bristol, Rhode Island was the source of the Taunton, Massachusetts information; all that was recorded was Bristol, Rhode Island. But Taunton, Massachusetts is in Bristol County.

Although that one mystery seemed solved, two other mysteries surrounded Daniel Landon. The first had to do with his wives. J. O. Landon, in his book, simply wrote "He married Ann ___." Truman Landon, in his genealogy, cited The Hartford Times for the information that "He married Ann and her sister Rebecca Lobdell." He also wrote that "Isaac Lobdell, father of Ann and Rebecca, mentions grandchildren Anne and Lydia Landon in his will."

It is questionable whether Daniel Landon married Ann and Rebecca Lobdell. In actuality, in his will, Isaac Lobdell wrote that his grandchildren were Anne and Lydia "Lendall". Vital Records of Hull, Massachusetts, where Isaac Lobdell lived, listed "Lidiah Landall md Mathew Loring" on February 5, 1718/19. While "Lendall" or "Landall" could have meant "Landon", it also could have meant "Lobdell".

45

Secondly, the only sources that have concluded that Isaac Lobdell had a daughter named Ann were the Landons. Lobdell genealogists never mentioned an Ann.

And thirdly, Rebecca Lobdell was born circa 1670, when Daniel Landon was 20 years old. She married Richard Stubbs circa 1690, when she was 20 years old. They had 10 children between June 10, 1692 and November 12, 1710. Richard died March 5, 1711 in Hull, Massachusetts, when Rebecca Lobdell was 41 years old. According to a 1989 NEGHR article on 17th century Hull by Ethel Farrington Smith, Rebecca married John Cox after Richard's death.

The other mystery concerned Daniel's life after 1689. The 1689 Bristol, Plymouth Colony census listed Daniel Landon living with one wife and seven children. While no later records have been found concerning him, it is known that at age 13 (1698) his son James was living with Daniel's brother Nathan in Southold, Long Island. From that time on, James was raised by Nathan.

And if Isaac's grandchildren mentioned in his will actually were Anne and Lydia Landon, were they singled out in his will because he had been raising them? But why were other people raising Daniel's children?

Ruth Cheney Ryan, a Landon researcher, proposed an intriguing possibility. At the same time that Daniel Landon disappeared from records, a Daniel Lander/Langley was arrested for piracy along with Thomas Pound. In Genealogical Guide to the Early Settlers of America, the Daniel "Langley" entry read "Boston, 1689, mariner, went with others that year to take a piratical ship in Vineyard Sound, of which in Geneal. Reg.II, 393, is account."

According to a 1689 record in the October, 1848, NEGHR, "Capne Samuel Pease comander set forth at Boston with the Colony of the Massachusetts Bay with Comission from the Governr and Council of the sd Colony bearing date the 30th day of September last past...to surprise and (in case of their resistance) by force of Armes to take Thomas Hawkins and Thomas Pound who with a number of armed men joyned with them had piratically seized severall Vessells belonging to their Maj'ties subjects of this Colony and other parts of the Country, &c."

Pound and his men were captured after a fight and arrested. In the July, 1891 NEGHR, Thomas Pound was considered again. Concerning his trial, the article read "These Examinants were convicted and executed". In Thomas Pound's first deposition in January, 1690, he stated "William Dunn, Daniel Lander, Samuel Watts and William Warren Examined Say, that these Examinants went in Company with Thomas Pounes and others in Thomas Hawkins his boat, lookt at Poune to be their Comandr and were along with him from the time of his going from Boston sometime in the beginning of August 1689, until the time they were taken by Captne Pease, and were belonging to him and assisting at the Seising and tobing of all the Vessells."

In records of the Court of Assistants of the Massachusetts Bay, "The said Daniel Lander to this Indictment pleaded not guilty and put himselfe upon Tryal by God and the Country. The Jury found said Daniel lander guilty of the Felony and piracy whereof he stands Indicted. The Court Adjudged the said Daniel Lander to have the sentence of death pronounced against him, (which was pronounced accordingly by the Deputy Governor). That is to say, That he said Daniel Lander be returned to the place from whence he came and from thence be carried to the place of Execution and there be hanged by the neck untill he be dead."

Most sources said Daniel was executed. However, in The Golden Age of Piracy, Ranker stated that in 1691, Thomas Pound was enlisted to help patrol coastal waters. His knowledge of the waters from Portsmouth, Maine to Virginia saved him from the gallows. Pound was given a commission in the Royal Navy and placed in command of the frigate, Dover Prize. He assumed command on April 17, 1691.

As previously stated, James, who was born March 29, 1685 to Daniel and his wife had been sent to live with his uncle Nathan Landon who was establishing himself as a leather worker and bricklayer in Southold, Long Island. Several Landon researchers have accepted James as Nathan's son. Although Nathan did have a son named James, his son died young.

He grew to be a cordwainer and blacksmith and he married Mary Vail, daughter of John, in 1707. They had Mary, Joseph, James, Daniel, Rachel and David. His wife Mary died in 1722 and was buried in the churchyard in Southold. The next year James married Mary Wilmont, a widow and the daughter of Francis Brown. They had Ann, Nathan and/or William. Mary Wilmont Landon died in 1753.

In A Short History of the Landon Family in America, Maynard H. Mires wrote that James belonged to the Southold Militia Company in 1715, under Benjamin Youngs.

In 1735, James was made a freeman and moved his family to Litchfield, Connecticut. He was a freeman juror there in 1737 and died there on September 19, 1738. His will was probated in Southold, Suffolk Co., New York and listed in 1738/39, Book II, page 115. He gave to his son James the house and land in Litchfield, to John 57 pounds, to Lydia and Ann 10 pounds each. His son Daniel was not mentioned.

James' son Daniel had been born on January 7, 1714 in Southold, Long Island, and probably moved to Litchfield, Connecticut, in 1735. His first wife may have been a Fiske of Brooklyn, New York. He married second to Martha Youngs of Southold on May 22, 1736. Both Southold and Litchfield claim the marriage in their records.

In 1741, Daniel was made freeman in Litchfield. In 1743, he was a voter; in 1746, he was a grand juror; and, in 1753, he became a selectman. On November 5, 1745, Daniel and twelve others organized the First Episcopal Society of Litchfield, later called St. Michael's Church, where he was parish clerk for 45 years. He deeded 50 acres of land to the society in 1747.

On November 2, 1771, the minister died and Daniel erected a monument in his memory. From 1777-80, Daniel and his family met regularly and Daniel read the service and sermon.

Maynard Mires, in his book, called Daniel "a man of sound intellect and extensive reading". J. O. Landon quoted records as saying "Capt. Daniel Landon officiated as lay reader, being always anxious to promote the welfare of the Church. All his family attended with him through 'honor and dishonor, through good report and evil report'."

As the rebellious mood in the colonies grew, the salary from the church ceased. Churchmen became unpopular. Anglicans were defamed, impeached and ridiculed. Their property was confiscated because they were suspected Loyalists. Catherine Crary, in <u>The Price of Loyalty</u>, wrote, "In almost every colony Tories were deliberately put to death, whether killed by a pitiless mob, murdered by a marauding party, hanged by a council of safety or assembly order or executed after court-martial proceedings."

Crary went on to write that "threats of ostracism and boycott, or mob mistreatment forced many to make an early decision when they would have preferred to drift along in an ambivalent way through the years of argument, even through the years of warfare". Such a problem may have been faced by Daniel's children as they watched when their church was attacked by an angry mob.

It must have been an especially difficult time for Daniel. One son, Daniel Jr., became a private for the colonists in the Revolutionary War and was listed in the DAR Patriot Index. His son Seth also supported the rebels as did Daniel's brother David in Southold. Many nephews; including Luther, son of James, and David, son of David; joined the Colonists.

But several of his sons, their families and many other Landons left the United States and emigrated to Canada because they supported the British and feared retaliation. Asa went to Augusta and Abner set-up a saw mill in Oswegatchie. King George gave Oliver Landon 200 acres on Lot 11, and 100 acres on each side of Kings Road, Leeds Co., Upper Canada.

According to Mires, after reading the Sunday morning service and sermon in St. Michael's, Daniel went home and died. He was buried in West Burying Ground, Litchfield, Connecticut. According to Mires, the verses on Daniel's tombstone had been composed by Daniel himself.

> Sacred to the memory of
> Daniel Landon of Litchfield
> Who died July 11, 1790, aged 77
> Who served as clerk to the Episcopal
> Church in Litchfield forty years.
>
> "His God he served with pious zeal
> The sacred dome was his delight
> For distant from this holy hill
> He took his everlasting flight.
>
> Lo here I leave this earthly clay
> And fly beyond the ethereal blue
> Unchained unto external day
> To sing the praise of God anew."

Chapter 10

Moore Family

Thomas I
    b. 1600; England
    m. Ann (d. aft 1636)
    d. 1636; Salem, Massachusetts
    Children
        Thomas (see below)
        Mary - m. Joseph Grafton of Salem

Thomas II
    b. Southwold, Suffolk Co., England
    m1. Martha Youngs; Reydon, Suffolk County, England
    m2. Catherine; Southold, Long Island
    d. June 27, 1691; Southold, Long Island
    Children
        Nathaniel (see below)
        Thomas III - b. August 21, 1639; Salem, Massachusetts
            bapt. - October 21, 1639; Salem, Massachusetts
            m. _____ Mott of Mamaroneck, New York
            Children
                Thomas - b. 1663
                Martha - m. John Peck
                Nathaniel
                Elisa
        Martha - bapt. October 21, 1639
            m. Captain John Symons
        Benjamin - b. June 2, 1640; Salem, Massachusetts
            bapt. August 2, 1640; Salem, Massachusetts
            m. Anne
            d. 1691
        Hannah - b. October 29, 1644; Salem, Massachusetts
            bapt. December 29, 1644; Salem, Massachusetts
            m. Rev. John Storrs and/or Symons; December
            17, 1667; Southold, Long Island
            d. Trenton
        Elizabeth - b. November 31, 1646; Salem,
            Massachusetts
            bapt. August 3, 1647; Salem, Massachusetts
            m. Simon Glover
        Jonathan - b. April 3, 1649; Salem; Massachusetts
            bapt. June 3, 1649; Salem Massachusetts
        Mary - b. December 15, 1650; Salem, Massachusetts
        Sarah - m. Samuel, son of Charles Glover

Nathaniel
    b. May 3, 1642; Salem, Massachusetts
    bapt. July 3, 1642; Salem, Massachusetts
    m. Sarah, dau of Jeremiah Vail
    Children
        Elizabeth - b. June 10, 1679; Southold, Long Island
            m. Christopher Youngs; c. 1697; Southport, Long
            Island
            d. February 22, 1747/48; Jamesport, Long Island
            will probated March 18, 1747/48

The first Thomas Moore was born in England; possibly in the
Southwold, Suffolk County area, before 1600. By 1631, Thomas I,
his wife Ann, and his daughter Mary, were in Salem,
Massachusetts and Thomas I was made a freeman. He died in Salem

in 1636, the year Harvard College was founded. The next year
his widow Ann, a midwife, was given a grant of land.

Thomas Moore II was born circa 1615 in Southwold, England.
There he met and married his first wife, Martha Youngs. She was
the daughter of Rev. Christopher Youngs of Reydon and Southwold,
Suffolk County, England, and the sister of Rev. John and Capt.
Joseph Youngs, later of Southold, Long Island.

Martha's brother Joseph was shipmaster of the "Love".
Thomas and Martha Youngs Moore left England in 1635 with Joseph,
Joseph's wife, and Christopher Youngs, Jr. Possibly they
traveled on Joseph's ship.

By July, 1636, Thomas and Martha were granted land in
Salem. In 1639, Thomas was listed as a member of the Salem
Church. He became a freeman on December 27, 1642.

On October 21, 1639, their first two children, Thomas III
and Martha, were baptized. Other children followed shortly.
Benjamin was born in 1640, Nathaniel in 1642, Hannah in 1644,
Elizabeth in 1646, Jonathan in 1649. All were born in Salem.
Two other children may have resulted from this marriage. A
daughter, Sarah, was mentioned in Thomas' will. In Youngs
Family, Selah Youngs added another daughter, Mary, born in Salem
on December 15, 1650. According to Colonial Families of the
United States, although Thomas was listed as a resident of
Southold, Long Island in 1650, his wife and children did not
join him in the wilderness until 1651. Possibly Martha remained
behind in order to have the child Selah Youngs claimed was born
in December, 1650 in Salem.

Sometime after moving to Southold, Martha died. According
to Long Island Genealogies, Thomas was married for the second
time to Catherine. There were no children by that marriage.

Although in Southold, Thomas Moore was a shipbuilder; it
might not have been his trade in England. Elpher Whitaker, in
his Southold history wrote "Thomas Moore was a ship builder and
owner, and one of the most prominent and wealthy men in
Southold, holding offices as constable, deputy, and magistrate.
He owned extensive property in all sections of town. In
addition, he owned property in Greenport, northeast of
Southold."

In 1659, Thomas bought the home of John Underhill in
Southold. On September 29, 1666, the family moved again when
Thomas purchased the home of Lt. John Ketcham and his wife,
Susan. Early parts of the house were built before 1658 and
consisted of an east front room, plus one other room. Town
Creek ran along the east of the property. Most additions to the
house - a parlor, keeping room and kitchen wing - were added in
the 1700's. A large central chimney opened into three
fireplaces.

That home became the sight of an important event in the
history of Southold. The Dutch, who had a stronghold on the
opposite end of Long Island, frequently tried to take over the
English end. On November 7, 1673, Dutch troops including 60
foot soldiers marched into Southold. Angry crowds defied their
Dutch invaders and refused allegiance. A battle seemed
inevitable. Dutch officers went to Magistrate Thomas Moore's
home. There they told him they wanted to appoint him to the

50

office of liaison between the Southolders and the Dutch. Thomas refused. When it became obvious that no one in the town would cooperate, more Dutch troops were sent to that end of Long Island, but they were always repulsed. Under Dutch occupation, residents of Southold, Southampton, and Easthampton avoided hostilities, but maintained their independence and continued with their English form of government. A treaty signed in 1674 restored the towns to English control.

On May 15, 1671, Thomas Moore and his wife Martha may have taken her niece's son, James Petty, to raise. However, since Martha died the next month, it was more likely Thomas III who took in young Petty.

In **English Origins of New England Families from the New England Historical and Genealogical Register** appeared the notation that Richard Browne was "bound to Thomas Moore 4 yeeres New England, Saphire Ketch" in 1679. This was probably the Thomas Moore of Southold.

On March 5, 1680, Thomas Moore gave "all my housing, lands and cattle, horse kinde, swine & sheep and Stoope, with all my moveables withing doors or without, to my son Nathaniel More he allowing his mother and father sufficient maintenance during their lives" (see Appendix IV). The deed was acknowledged by "john Yonge, Sherife". There was no explanation why he gave up everything a full eleven years before his death or why it was all given to Nathaniel when Thomas had two older children.

Thomas Moore's will was dated June 23, 1691 (see Appendix IV). He died shortly thereafter. In his will he left his second wife, Catherine, "One-third of all my goods, lands, commages and meado lands, dwelling houses, barns, orchards, garden fences..." He named Thomas as his eldest son and Nathaniel as his third son. Daughters mentioned were Martha, Hannah, Elizabeth and Sarah.

Thomas and Mary's son, Nathaniel, was born May 3, 1642, in Salem and baptized July 3, 1642, in Salem Church. He married Sarah, daughter of Jeremiah Vail and his first wife Catherine, in Southold, Long Island. When his father died, Nathaniel inherited all the lands, houses and buildings his father had owned "between Wm Wells & Tomms Creek head". Nathaniel died in Southold, Long Island on June 10, 1733.

Nathaniel's daughter, Elizabeth, was born June 10, 1679, in Southold, Long Island. She was married circa 1697 to Christopher Youngs (1675-1727), son of Christopher, grandson of Christopher and great-grandson of Rev. John Youngs. Elizabeth's son Daniel was born in 1712, in Aqueboque, Long Island. Her daughter Martha Youngs married Daniel Landon on May 22, 1736.

Elizabeth died February 22, 1749 at the age of 68 years, 8 months, and 8 days in Jamesport, Long Island. Her will was listed in Book III, page 82 of the New York Calendar of Wills. Her son, Christopher, was appointed administrator of her estate.

Chapter 11

Paine / Payne Family

Thomas
    b.c. 1541
    m. Katherine (d. May 18, 1620), dau of Thomas Harssant of
    Cransford; Suffolk Co., England; June 2, 1578
    d. April 14, 1631; Blything, Suffolk Co., England
    Children
        Thomas (see below)
        Henri - b. 1579
            d. 1579
        John - b. 1580
        Maria - b. 1583
        Robarte - b. 1584

Thomas
    b. December 11, 1586; Wrenton, Suffolk Co., England
    m. Elizabeth, dau of Henry Tuthill of Tharston, Norfolk
    Co., England; November 22, 1610
    d. by 1640
    will dated April 10, 1638; Salem, Massachusetts
    Children
        Peter (see below)
        Mary - b. October 12, 1611; Suffolk Co. England
            m. Philemon Dickinson (d. by 1672; Southold, Long
            Island), 1639
            Children
                Peter - m. Mary Folger
                Thomas
                Mary
                Elizabeth
        Thomas - b. January 18, 1612/13; Suffolk Co., England
            m. Rebecca Peck (will dated March 3, 1687/8);
            April 25, 1671; Dedham, Massachusetts
            d. September 6, 1686
            will dated July 26, 1686
            Children
                Rebecca - b. September 19, 1642
                    m. Thomas Patten; February 1, 1662;
                    Dedham, Massachusetts
                Thomas - bapt. March 24, 1644
                John - b. April 27, 1646
                    m. Elizabeth Hunting; April 18, 1671
        Elizabeth - b. January 20, 1614/15; Suffolk
            Co., England
        Dorothy - b. December 6, 1618; Suffolk Co.,
            England
        John - m. August 25, 1620; Suffolk Co.
            England
            m. Sarah
            d. Southold, Long island
        Sarah - b. March 7, 1621; Suffolk Co.,
            England
        Nathaniel - b. July 21, 1626
            d. 1636

Peter
    b. March 14, 1616/17; Wentrom, Suffolk Co., England
    m. Mary Folger
    d. by September 15, 1658; Southold, Long island

Many of the early settlers of Southold originated in Suffolk Co. England. Thomas Paine, the earliest listed in this line, lived most of his life in Blything in Suffolk Co., England. On June 20, 1578, he married Catharine (Katherine), daughter of Thomas "Harssant" of Cransford near Framlingham in Suffolk Co.

Their son Thomas II married Elizabeth Tuthill on November 22, 1610 and had Mary, Thomas, Elizabeth, Dorothy, Sarah, Nathaniel, Peter and John. According to Lists of Emigrants to America 1600-1700, between April 13, 1637 and May 10, 1637, Thomas Paine, a 50-year-old weaver from Wrenton, along with his 53-year-old wife and 6 children, requested permission to emigrate to Salem. The children listed were "Thomas: John: Marey: Elizabeth: Dorothey: and Sarah."

The family finally emigrated aboard the "Mary Anne" out of Yarmouth on June 20, 1637. Nathaniel and Peter did not accompany their parents. Nathaniel had died the previous year. Peter, who was 20 years old when his parents emigrated may have preceded or followed his parents.

Thomas' family settled in Salem where, in 1638, Thomas II wrote his will. He died in Salem by 1640.

Thomas III was made a freeman in 1641. The John Paine listed as a freeman in Connecticut or the one listed as a proprietor of New Haven in 1685 may have been Thomas II's son and/or grandson. Several other members of the family settled in Dedham, Massachusetts.

Peter married Mary Folger and settled in Southold, Long Island. In September, 1652, Peter paid a debt to the estate of Capt. Robert Button of Suffolk Co., Massachusetts. He died in Southold, Long Island, by age 41. His estate, inventoried on September 15, 1658; was worth over 70 pounds (see Appendix V). The appraisers were Barnabas Horton, William Pierrier and Charles Glover; and "Mary, the late wife of Peter Payne," acknowledged it.

Chapter 12

Sylvester Family

Unknown, brother of "Jeofrie" Sylvester of St. James, Duke's
Place, London, England
     m. Mary (d. aft 1657)
     Children
          Nathaniel (see below)
          Giles - b.c. 1630
               m. Anne (b.c. 1644), dau of Sir Redmayne Burrell
               of Dowsby, Lincoln Co. England; January 13,1662;
               Great St. Bartholomew, London, England
               d. London, England
               will proved May 26, 1671
          Constant - m. Grace, sister of Henry Walrond
               d. 1671, Barbadoes
               Children
                    Humphrey - d. April, 1673
                    Constant
                    Grace
                    Mary
          Mary - m. Isaac Cartwright (d. prior to 1671)
               Children
                    Constant
                    Anne
                    Mary
          Peter - m. Mary, dau of Thomas and Anne Wase Brinley
               d. 1657; London, England
               will proved February 11, 1657
          Daughter - m. _____ Kett
               Children - Richard
          Joshua

Nathaniel
     m. Grizzell (bapt. January 6, 1635/6; St James Church,
     Clerkenwell, England) dau of Thomas (d. October 15, 1661)
     and Anne Wase Brinley of Datchett, Buckinghamshire,
     England;
     sis of Francis Brinley
     d. March, 1680; Shelter Island, New York
     Children
          Nathaniel - m. Margaret, dau of Capt. Josiah Hobart of
               Easthampton, Long Island
               d. aft 1705
               will dated April 3, 1700
               codicil dated April 24, 1705
               Children
                    Brinley - b.c. 1693
                         m. Mary (c. 1702-1705)
                         d. December 24, 1752
                    Nathaniel
                    Margaret
                    Grizzell
          Mercy - d. young
          Grizzell - m. James Lloyd (1650-1693) who m2 Rebecca,
               dau of Gov. John and Sarah Sedwick Leverett); c.
               1670
               d. by November, 1691
               Children
                    Henry - m. Rebecca, dau of John Nelson
                    Joseph
                    James

Grizzell
Giles - m. Hannah, dau of Thomas Savage; September,
  1685
Peter - m. Elizabeth
  d.c. 1695
Constant - will dated October 26, 1695
  d. 1696
Patience - b. aft 1659
  m. Benjamin L'Hommedieu
  Children
    Susana - b.c. 1704
        m. Jonathan Tuthill; February 27, 1723
        d. May 16, 1743
    Sylvester
    Benjamin
Elizabeth - b. aft 1659
  m. Jonathan Brown
Mary - b. aft 1659
Ann - b. aft 1659
Mercy - b. aft 1659
Benjamin - b. aft 1659
  d.c. 1689

In _Genealogical Dictionary_, Savage wrote that Nathaniel
could not, as had been suggested, have been the son of Joshua
Sylvester, translator of Du Barta's rhapsodies. The connection
was first suggested because Nathaniel did have a brother named
Joshua.

Everything that could be determined about Nathaniel's
ancestry came from relatives' wills. In his 1657 London will,
Nathaniel's brother Peter left 25 pounds to "my uncle Jeofrie
Silvester", 15 pounds to "my cousin Joseph Gascoigne," and 5
pounds each to "Aunt Gascoigne...and to her daughter Anne
Gascoigne" and refers to his "dear mother Mary Silvester of
London, widow."

Peter Sylvester married Mary and Nathaniel married
Grizzell, daughters of Thomas and Anne Wase Brinley. According
to _Genealogical Gleanings_, Thomas Brinley was "one of the
auditors of the Revenue of King Charles the First and of King
Charles the Second" and son of Richard and Joane Reeve Brinley
of Willenhall. Thomas Brinley's will was dated September 13,
1661 in Datchett in Buckinghamshire. His eldest son, Francis
Brinley, inherited two thirds of the manor of Burton in
Yorkshire and "tnements in the town of Newcastle upon Tyre."
Thomas also bequeathed land and the manor of Wakerfield, and
lands in the "counties of Middlesex an Bucks." He also
bequeathed a legacy to his daughter Mary Silvester and
granddaughter Mary Silvester who were "both left destitute of
subsistence by the decease of ...daughter's late husband, Peter
Silvester."

Nathaniel was the first proprietor of Shelter Island under
a grant from Charles II in 1666. Originally called Manhansack-
Ahaqua-Shuwamock, or variations of that, depending upon the
source, the island was the land of the Manhansett tribe. The
Indian name meant "an island sheltered by island" - a perfect
description. It lay between Long Island's northern and southern
peninsulas, an equal distance from Southold and Easthampton, at
the outlet of Peconic Bay. The island was dotted with small bays
and coves. The six mile by four mile island belonged to
Southold until 1730 when it was incorporated into a separate

township. According to Thompson, the island's "offices were formerly chosen, taxes assessed, and other matters in relation to the island (were) transacted at the annual town meetings in Southold; consequently there are no separate records to be found here anterior to 1730."

Nathaniel, along with his brother Constant, Thomas Middleton, and Thomas Rouse; paid 1600 pounds of Muscovado sugar to Stephen Goodyeare. According to Thompson's, Long Island History, Goodyeare was "an extensive and opulent merchant of New Haven." Goodyeare had purchased both Shelter and Robin's Island from James Farrett, an agent of William, the Earl of Stirling, on May 18, 1641. The grantees also procured an agreement with the local Indian chiefs, allowing the English to live in peace on the island.

On May 8, 1656, Thomas Rouse sold his part of the island to John Booth who transferred it to Nathaniel Sylvester who gave a portion of it to Constant Sylvester, his brother, on September 12, 1662. When the English took jurisdiction over the island, the owners asked Gov. Nicoll for a "perpetual exemption from taxes." The governor declared it a town with the same "privileges and immunites" and requested one lamb per year for taxes, deliverable May 1st of each year.

When the Dutch recaptured the area in 1673, they confiscated the interest in the island belonging to Thomas Middleton and Constant Sylvester, supposedly as a punishment for taking part in the war against the Dutch. On August 28, 1674, the interests formerly belonging to Middleton and Constant were sold to Nathaniel Sylvester, making him sole owner of Shelter Island.

However neither Thomas Middleton nor Constant Sylvester had ever been resident owners. Since Constant was a London merchant living in Barbadoes and may never have ever visited New England or seen Shelter Island, his supposed participation in the war against the Dutch was questionable. In his April 7, 1671 will, Constant left his share of Shelter Island to, first, his sons Constant and Humphrey; and, then, to his brother Joshua; and, finally, to Nathaniel. Since Constant, Jr., Humphrey and Joshua died without children, Constant's share would have finally gone to Nathaniel's heir even without the Dutch confiscation.

Nathaniel wrote in his will that the island became his because of "the great disbursements made by me...in their (Thomas and Constant's) behalf since the year 1652 until this present year (1680)" and "money which my brother Constant doth in particular stand indebted unto me." Those debts may have been, in part, connected with the need to buy back the partners' portions of Shelter Island or with events during that time. For instance, after the Dutch had taken New York, the commanders sent a man-of-war to Shelter Island. According to Nathaniel, the captain and a fifty soldier landing party landed, threatened the Sylvesters and demanded money.

Sylvester Manor was built at the northern end of the island. The burial ground, probably the oldest on the island, no longer holds the stones of the Sylvesters. Most were moved to the churchyard near the center of the island.

However, engravings at the table tomb at the manor showed why Shelter Island was a perfect name for the place (see

Appendix VI). Although they were Puritans, Nathaniel and, later, his son Giles took up the cause of the Quakers. Listed on the table tomb were the names of those who had found shelter on the island: including George Fox, "founder of the Society of Quakers"; Mary Dyer, William Robinson, William Leddra, and Marmaduke Stevenson who were executed on Boston Common. The tablet listed others who were tortured and referred to Giles Sylvester as "The Champion". Savage described it as "the more enduring worth of bold service in the higher cause of humanity shall be accorded to him who gave protection and shelter to the Shattuck and Southwick fugitives from the bloody persecution in Massachusetts under the successive rule of Govs Endicott and Bellingham, whose zeal for the honor of God exterminated all tenderness for their fellow creatures."

At the time of Nathaniel's will, proven October 2, 1680, most of his children were minors and bequests would go to them "at age of twenty-one or marriage." Under age twenty-one were Patience, Elizabeth, Mary, Ann, Mercy, Nathaniel and Peter. Sons Giles, Constant and Benjamin were also mentioned in the will. Sons Peter and Nathaniel inherited "certain bricks lying at Thomas Moore Senior's farm and at Oyster Bay. Nathaniel asked that his "children to be brought up in the fear of God, and to have such education bestowed upon them as may be conveniently gotten in these parts of the world, and as shall seen neet to my endeared wife, their mother." Nathaniel provided for his brother Joshua "to be conveniently maintained with diet, lodging, clothing and necessaries, decent and becoming his as hither to he hath enjoyed, that he may in no manner or way want, and in no wise put off from the Island, unless he shall think good to live elsewhere" Nathaniel also mentioned property he owned in Southold and "Roberts" Island. Executors of the estate were wife Grizzell, brother-in-law Francis Brinley, son-in-law James Lloyd, cousin Isaac Arnold, Levi Morris and Daniel Gould.

Thompson wrote that Benjamin L'Hommedieu who married Patience, Nathaniel Sylvester's daughter, was a Huguenot from La Rochelle, France, who had fled to Holland when faced with the threatened repeal of the Edict of Nantes.

James Lloyd, who married Nathaniel's daughter Grizzell, owned land "near the town of Osterbay, known by the name Horseneck, and also two thirds of a neck of meadow to the South side of Long Island called Fort neck." In his will, Lloyd named his wife, Francis Brinley and John Nelson as executors. According to Genealogical Gleanings in England, Nelson was a prisoner, first, in Quebec; then, in Chateau d'Angouleme in France; and, finally, in the Bastille. His crimes were not recorded.

Although Nathaniel's son Nathaniel owned land on Shelter Island, he moved to Rhode Island. His April 3, 1700 will; which was witnessed by "James Brading, Matthias Burn, John Marry and Abiel Caril," and had a 1705 codicil appointing Benjamin Newberry and Arnold Collins as executors; was proven in Rhode Island on July 4, 1705. But it indicated he lived in Easthampton, Long Island. His son Brinley Sylvester inherited what was left of his father's share of Shelter Island. According to Thompson, in 1737, Brinley moved from Rhode Island to Shelter Island, where he "built a stately mansion" and died in 1752.

Nathaniel's son Benjamin, Constant and Peter all died without issue. So their shares all went to Giles who ended up with four-fifths of the island. In 1659 Giles sold one-fifth of the island to William Nicoll of Islip. However, Giles also died without children and, by his 1730 will, left his land to Nicoll.

In 1730, Brinley Sylvester, Nathaniel Jr's. son, contested the will of Giles Sylvester. However, according to Thompson, "the governor and council decided in favor of 'Nicoll'."

It was interesting that Gile's will was contested since, in 1695, Giles, then proprietor of Shelter Island, petitioned Col. William Smith, Judge of the Prerogative Court, for more time "to prove his allegations why ye last Will of his late Brother Peter Sylvester ought not be proved." Giles had already had one extension. According to the inventory, Peter's worth was 216 pounds 17 shillings 7 pence and his wife was to inherit.

Chapter 13

Tuttle / Tuthill Family

Henry
     b. Tharston, Norfolk Co. England
     Children
          Henry II(see below)
          Elizabeth - b.c. 1584
               m. Thomas Paine; November 22, 1610; England
               d. 1650; Salem, Massachusetts
               Children
                    Peter   John
                    Mary   Elizabeth
                    Thomas   Dorothy
                    Sarah   Nathaniel
          John - m1. Unknown
               m2. Weybred, Suffolk Co., England

Henry II
     b. Tharston, Norfolk Co., England
     m. Bridget (d. by 1650)
     d.c. 1644
     Children
          John (see below)
          Elizabeth - m. William Johnson

John
     b. July 16, 1635; England
     m. Deliverance King; February 17, 1657; Southold, Long
     Island
     d. 1683; Oyster Pond, Long Island
     will inventoried September 12, 1683
     Children
          Henry III (see below)
          John - b. February 14, 1659
               m1. Mehitable, dau of Mary Wells Mapes
               m2. Sarah Youngs; May 28, 1690
               will probated 1743
               Children
                    James - d. Cutchogue, Long Island
                    Joshua - d. Cutchogue, Long Island
                    John
                    Daniel
          Daniel - b. January 23, 1680
               will probated 1763
               Children
                    Nathaniel
                         Children
                              Nathaniel - dau of Gideon and
                                   Rachel Rackett Youngs; August
                                   7, 1755
                    Daniel Jr.
                         Children
                              Nathaniel
          Nathaniel - b. November 10, 1683
          Abigail - m. Joseph Conkling; November, 1690;
               Southold, Long Island
          Elizabeth
          Hannah
          Dorothy

```
            Deliverance

Henry III
     Children
          Jonathan - b.c. 1691
               m. Susanna L'Hommedieu (b.c. 1704-1743); February
               23, 1723
               d. February 8, 1741/2
               Children
                    Benjamin - b.c. 1725
                         d. February 16, 1748/9
          Henry IV
               Children
                    Henry V
                         Children
                              Anna - m. Rev. Timothy Symmes
                                   (1742-1814)
                                   Children
                                        Anna - b. Southold, Long
                                        Island
                                        m. President
                                        William Henry
                                        Harrison;
                                        November 22, 1795
                                        d. February 25,
                                        1864
```

According to an 1867 address given by William H. Tuttle, the family descended from the O'Toole family of Wicklow and Kildare Counties, Ireland. Tuttle claimed that the Tuthill/O'Toole names were interchangeable in ancient records and that the name came down from an early Irish king named Tuathal.

William Tuttle stated that in 1230, Thomas de Touthel paid an annual rent of 8 shillings in Yorkshire. "Tothill" appeared in early records in Devonshire. Richard Tottell of Wales became a famous printer during the reigns of Elizabeth and James. "Toothills" lived in Yorkshire and Totehill Manor was built in Cambridgeshire.

In the 1400's, the Tuthills of Norfolk Co. settled in Saxlingham, seven miles south of Norwich. William Tuttle wrote that after 1585, younger family members moved - some to Heigham Lodge near Norwich, some to Essex, and some to Suffolk near Rev. John Youngs' English home. Banks' Topographical Dictionary listed a Henry Tuttle as emigrating from Fressingfield, Suffolk Co. to Hingham, Massachusetts. However, Savage concurred with the accepted view that Henry originated in Norfolk.

The first Henry Tuthill in this genealogy was from Tharston, Norfolk Co., England. Oddly enough, Tharston was only about 10 miles southwest of Norwich, quite near where the Folger family lived in England. At least two of his children, Henry II and Elizabeth, emigrated permanently to the New World; and one son, John, emigrated for a short period.

Henry I's daughter Elizabeth married Thomas Paine and emigrated with her husband and six children in 1637. Her husband died in Salem in 1650. Her son Peter, later, married Mary Folger and settled in Southold, Long Island.

Henry II was probably accompanied to New England in 1637 by his brother John, a widower. Later, John returned to England where he married for a second time and settled in Weybred, Suffolk Co.

But before leaving the Colonies, John did some area surveying in Southold. April 6, 1642 New Haven town records reported "John Touttle of Yennycock (Southold) deputed by the Court to be Constable to order the affayers of that plantation the time being till some further course be taken by this Court for the setting of a Magistrate according to God." The position of constable was the chief executive officer and, with elected overseers, conducted the town's affairs. That was probably the same John that William Tuttle was discussing when he stated that "On the 17th March 1644, the Colony Constitution was revised and enlarged; and then were added to it names of Matthew Rowe and John Tuthill."

Henry II was given a land grant and settled in Hingham, Massachusetts. Town records indicated he was granted "several parsalls of land and meadow" - 9 acres for planting, a 4-acre home lot, and 4 3/4 other acres. The home lot was "butting up on Batchelor Streett (sic), eastward bounded with the land of William Large, westward; with the land Jonathan Bosworth, northward; and with the land of Thomas Chafin southward." He was a freeman in Hingham in March, 1638 and a constable in 1640.

However, on June 20, 1644, he sold his home lot and "Conihasset meadows" to John Ferring. His name did not appear again in Hingham records. Either he moved to Southold, Long Island, and died shortly thereafter or he died shortly before his family moved to Southold.

Henry II had at least two children, John and Elizabeth. Township records (Book A fo 105) dated December 15, 1650, indicated John's mother Bridget had married William Wells of Southold after her husband's death. When Bridget died, legal guardianship of the children had gone to Wells. In the 1650 document, with his mother having died, John gave any claim he had on his father's and uncle's estates to Wells (see Appendix VII). No reason for the action was given. The document was witnessed by Pastor John Youngs and Marie Wells. Additional General Court proceedings of May 31, 1654 were concerned with the controversy over the children's inheritances.

But when John married Deliverance King three years later, he had already acquired a good deal of land, including land at Oyster Pond. Later, in 1776, a fort was built there to prevent the landing of British troops on that branch of the island.

Thompson, in _History of Long Island_, wrote that John, Henry II's son, died in 1717, at the age of 82. But he was more likely the John Tuttle, Sr. whose inventory appeared in "Early Probate Records of New Haven". That estate was inventoried September 12, 1683 by John Cooper, Sr. and John Winston and valued at 79 pounds 1 shilling. John would have been 48 years old. His last child, Nathaniel was born just 2 months later. His son John Jr. who was born in 1659 may have been the John who died in 1717 at age 58. And the Elizabeth Tuttle whose estate was inventoried on February 3, 1684 may have been John Sr.'s daughter.

Thompson reported John Jr. represented the county at the Colonial Assembly from 1 94-1698. John Tuttle, Jr. married Sarah Youngs on May 28, 1690. Sarah was his second wife. He had four sons; John III, James, Joshua and Daniel. William Tuttle reported that John III was known as "Chalker John" and became Justice of the Peace. He described John III "possessing great natural shrewdness, and energy of character, combined with affability of manner and sterling honesty, he became a great favorite with the people, and held various offices of trust and responsibility." William related he was a commissioner who helped lay out the "Kings Highway" from Brooklyn to Easthampton and, in 1693, was a member of the colonial legislature of New York.

Another of John Sr.'s sons, Henry, had a son named Jonathan who married Susanna L'Hommedieu. Susanna was born circa 1704 to Benjamin and Patience (Sylvester) L'Hommedieu. Patience, daughter of Nathaniel Sylvester of Shelter Island, had Benjamin circa 1725. Jonathan, Susanna and Benjamin were buried in the Old Orient Point Burying Ground, a cemetery located between Orient Harbor and Long Island Sound. The cemetery was situated west of Orient, the village originally named Oyster Pond.

Chapter 14

Underhill Family

John Underhill (Capt.)
 b. 1597, England
 m1. Helena Kruger (d. by 1658), Holland
 m2. Elizabeth (1633-1674/5), dau of Lt. Robert and
 Elizabeth Fones Winthrop Feake (Feke)
 d. July 21, 1672; Oyster Bay, Long Island
 Children
  Nathaniel (see below)
  Benoi - b. 1629
   m. Chloe Beverly
   Children
    John - b. 1657
     Children
      Sampson - b. 1697
       m. Elizabeth Ambrose (b.1698)
       d. 1732
  Elizabeth - bapt. 1636
   m. Isaac Smith
  John - b. April 11, 1642
   bapt. April 24, 1642
   m. Mary (1625-98), dau of Matthew and Mary Prior
   d. December 25, 1692
   Children
    John - b. 1670
     m1. Elizabeth (1674-1713), dau of
      Thomas
     (1650-1710) and Dinah Willets
     m2. Susannah Birsall
     d. May, 1728
     Children
      Thomas - b. 1702
       m. Sarah Powell (1710-1792)
      Amos - m. Elizabeth, dau of
       Benjamin and Jane Mott
       Seamen; 1729; Long Island
      Mary
      Deborah
      Isaac
      Daniel
    Daniel - b. 1672
    Samuel - b. 1674
     d. young
    Mary - b. 1677
     m. Wright (1676-1738), son of William
     (d. 1719) and Rebecca Wright
     Frost
     d. 1751
    Abraham - b. 1679
     m. Sarah, dau of Thomas Townsend
    Deborah - b. 1682
    Samuel - b. 1685
     m. Hannah, dau of Thomas and Dinah
     Willets; 1700
     Children
      Anne
      Dinah
      Samuel
      Abraham
    Sarah - b. 1687

```
                    m. Thomas Persall, 1708
              Jacob - b. 1689
                    m. Mary Wright, dau of John and Mary
                    Townsend
              Hannah - b. 1690
                    m. Thomas, son of Samuel Browne; 1716
         Deborah - b. 1659/60; Oyster Bay, Long Island
              m. Henry Townsend (d. 1695) of Oyster Bay
              Children
                    Henry - d. 1709
                          m. Eliphal Wright
                          Children
                                Henry - m. Elizabeth Titus (b.
                                1699)
         Hannah - b. 1666
              m. Thomas, son of Richard Alsop
              d. 1751
         David - b. 1672
              m. Hannah


Nathaniel
    b. 1663
    m. Mary, dau of John and Mary Ferris of Throckmorton Neck;
    1685
    d. 1710
    Children
         Nathaniel - b. 1690
              m. Mary Honeywell
         Benjamin - b. 1694
              m. Hannah
              Children
                    John - b. 1719
                          m. Sarah Thorne
                          d. 1784
                          Children
                                Isaac
         Abraham - b. 1697
              m. Hannah Cromwell
              d. 1758
              Children
                    Abraham - b. 1723
                          m1. Phebe Hallock
                          m2. Kaziah of Farrington, Connecticut;
                          1746
                          d. 1789
                    Isaac - m. Sarah Field, 1756
                          Children
                                Caleb
                    Jacob - m. Amy Hallock, 1747
                          Children
                                Samuel - m. Martha Quimby
              Martha
              Hannah
              Mary
         Thomas - m. Phebe Davenport
```

Captain John Underhill would be called a "character" if he
were alive today. While his early years were sketchy, all
sources have agreed he was born circa 1597 in England. Bank's
Topographical Dictionary put Underhill's origin as Kenilworth in
Warwickshire Co., England. He may have named one of his Long
Island homes "Kenilworth" for a time. Or he could have been the
son of John Underhill, the third son of Edward of Ettington and

grandson of John of Wolverhampton by his second wife Agnes, daughter and heir of Thomas Porter. Burke's Landed Gentry agreed with Ettington as a possible origin and suggested John may have been the brother of Thomas and Clement Underhill of circa 1634 London. Thompson's History of Long Island, and Bodges' Soldiers in King Philip's War indicated Underhill served in Ireland and at Cadiz. However, Bodges wrote that he served with the Dutch Army there while Thompson argued it was the British Army.

Whatever his origin, John Underhill was among the 900 emigrants who went to Boston with John Winthrop. The Winthrop Fleet arrived in 1630. His wife, the former Helen Kruger of Holland, joined him on December 15, 1633. His daughter Elizabeth was baptized on February 14, 1636 and his son John, Jr. on April 24, 1642.

The Abridged Compendium listed Underhill as "a financier of the Mayflower." The Compendium also asserted that Underhill arrived in the Colonies in 1628. It is known he was in Boston before May, 1631, when he became a freeman. He joined the First Church of Boston, becoming the 57th member on the list; served as deputy to Boston's General Court in 1634; was captain of the training band in 1636; and was the first person to command the Boston militia.

Underhill was on the treasurer records of Massachusetts as early as 1632 when he was granted a thirty-pound-a-year pension "for services rendered to the colony." Underhill and Daniel Patrick had conducted military training sessions. A fifty pound tax had been levied in 1630 to support Underhill and Patrick. The grant referred to in 1632 may have been connected to the training program. Or those services may have been some other military services, for that was Underhill's primary undertaking for the remainder of his life.

Although Bodge blamed the Pequot War on the Pequot's cruelty, John Underhill may well have been an instigator. Sir Henry Vane, the governor of Massachusetts and a friend of Underhill's, put together ninety men divided into four groups commanded by Underhill, Nathaniel Turner, William Jennison and Richard Davenport with John Endicott over them all. Underhill's group was sent to Block Island as a reprisal for the murder of John Oldham.

When they landed on August 31, 1636, they were met by 40 braves with only bows and arrows to defend themselves. The braves fled immediately. After two days of futile searching for the Indians, Underhill and his men burnt the wigwams, destroyed the Indians' corn, wrecked seven canoes and killed one Indian. After being reinforced at Saybrook Fort by Lt. Lion Gardiner, the group went out to "hunt" Indians again. They found no Indians, but did destroy more wigwams. They arrived back in Boston in September with no losses.

To the Pequots, these acts meant a declaration of war. Saybrook's garrison, led by Lt. Gardiner, was in a serious situation. The fort was under siege for many months before Capt. Underhill and a company of twenty men were sent as reinforcements in April, 1637.

Later, Underhill was wounded in the hip and another arrow hit his helmet at the battle at the Naragansett fort . After the battle, Capt. Mason and the able-bodied men marched overland while Underhill and the other wounded returned by boat to Saybrook. Shortly after, with their tour of duty at Saybrook ended, Underhill and his men returned to Massachusetts. In 1638, Underhill published a book in England titled News from America, or a New and Experimental Discoverie of New England; containing a true relation of warlike proceedings these two years past, with a figure of the Indian for or plaisade; by John Underhill, a commander in the warrs there, describing his exploits.

While his military abilities enhanced his status, a NEGHR editor called Underhill "a man of very eccentric character - an enthusiast in religion, but immoral in practice." Thompson, in History of Long Island, called him a "debaucher". The September 7, 1638 entry from Winthrop's famous journal discussed how, after being dealt with privately concerning Underhill's "incontinency with a neighbor's wife" and not refraining, Underhill was publicly questioned. Winthrop called the young Mrs. Faber "beautiful, and withal of a jovial spirit and behavior." The accusation was that Underhill went to Mrs. Faber's home everyday and was frequently found alone with her behind a locked door. As punishment, Underhill was condemned and banished.

Supposedly during his banishment, Underhill went to New Hampshire where; in 1638, he became the governor of Exeter and Dover. However, Savage wrote "the same infirmity render. his rem. from New Hampshire." And Thompson wrote "but his conduct [in New Hampshire] could not long be tolerated, on account of his great irregularity. He behaved very ungratefully even toward his wife..." However, in 1668, a Giles Underhill had a complaint lodged against him in New Hampshire for deserting his wife. Could Savage have confused Giles with John?

According to Winthrop, Underhill confessed to adultery in front of an assembly in Boston in 1639 (see Appendix VIII). However, the church ignored his pleas for forgiveness.

Next he moved to Stamford, Connecticut, where he became a delegate to the General Court at New Haven and was appointed an assistant justice. And in 1639, he asked the Dutch government to allow a few families onto Long Island. However, Underhill refused to agree to the terms suggested by the Dutch.

Shortly after his aborted attempt to settle on Long Island, Underhill was back in Boston confessing again to adultery with Mrs. Faber and attempting adultery with another woman. The church banished him yet again.

Finally, in 1640, when he confessed yet again, that time in course clothing, he was admitted to the church again. He was also required to ask the forgiveness.

In a letter written by Underhill to his friend Hansard Knowles and reproduced in History of Long Island, Underhill, while admitting he had also looked lustfully on Miriam Wilbore, wrote that most of his problems stemmed from his being connected with Anne Huchinson and her religious beliefs.

Of course the Puritan definition of "adultery" may not have had the same meaning as today. Perhaps that was why Savage related that Underhill was banished for heresy and Bodge claimed that Underhill was disfranchised because he did not accept civil or ecclesiastical authority and he sided with Anne Huchinson.

In 1644, Underhill and others went to Long Island and settled in Flushing, possibly at Dutch invitation. Eventually Underhill was employed by the Dutch to fight Indians in the New Amsterdam area. His Indian fighting led to Underhill obtaining a good estate on Long Island from the Dutch. He so transferred his allegiance that Underhill became a member of the Council of New Netherlands.

Then in 1653, Underhill was commissioned by Rhode Island to fight the Dutch. His quickly shifted loyalties sent him from working for the Dutch, to seizing Dutch lands for England (see Appendix VIII).

In 1654, Underhill was in the Southold, Long Island area. In 1657, he owned a house adjoining Joseph Youngs' home. His wife died soon after and, circa 1658, he married Elizabeth, daughter of either Henry Winthrop or, more likely, Lt. Robert Feake. According to Bunker, he sold his home to Thomas Moore in 1657.

Underhill received a land grant Oyster Bay, which he originally named Kenilworth. At Oyster Bay, Underhill joined the Society of Friends (Quakers). He was a delegate from Oyster Bay to a meeting in Hempstead called by Governor Nicoll. He was also made "sheriff of the north riding of Long Island" during that time.

Information that he disclosed concerning earlier arrangements made between the Dutch and the Indians, so irritated the Dutch that they sent a group of Dutch soldiers to take Underhill prisoner. But Underhill pled his loyalty to the Dutch and was allowed to go free.

He died at Oyster Bay on July 21, 1672. His September 18, 1671 will stipulated that his youngest son at the time, Nathaniel, had to remain with his mother Elizabeth until he reached age 21. He was eight years old when his father died. Another son was born after John Underhill's death. His son John, Jr. was made administrator of the will .

John Underhill lived a full life. Assuming the 1597 birthdate was correct; Underhill emigrated at age 31, his first child was born at age 32, and he continued to father children until his death at age 75. He commanded troops when he was in his 50's and was captured by the Dutch in his 60's. He lived in England; Holland,; Boston, Massachusetts; Saybrook, Connecticut; New Hampshire; and several places on Long Island, New York. Could that all be true?

If the 1597 birthdate was off by 10 years, Underhill's life would have made more sense. He would have emigrated at age 21, fathered his first child at 22, and fathered his last child at 65. The only problem was that Underhill had supposedly fought at Cadiz and in Ireland before emigrating.

A second possibility was that two John Underhill's had led this full life. Granted, one John Underhill could have done all the things described for him. If he did, John Underhill was definitely an extraordinary man.

Chapter 15

Vail Family

Jeremiah
>   b. 1618, England
>   m1. Catherine (d.c. March, 1659)
>   m2. Mary Folger Paine; May 24, 1660
>   d. 1687; Southold, Long Island
>   Children by Catherine
>>   Abigail - bapt. March 18, 1645; Salem, Massachusetts
>>   Sarah - bapt. March 21, 1646; Salem, Massachusetts
>>>   m. Nathaniel Moore
>>   Jeremiah - bapt. December 30, 1649
>>>   m1. Mary
>>>   m2. Anne, wid of Benjamin Moore (d. by 1691)
>   Children by Mary
>>   John (see below)
>>   David or Daniel - b. 1665; Southold, Long Island
>>   Mary - b. 1667; Southold, Long Island
>>>   d. September 22, 1689; Southold, Long Island

John
>   b. 1663; Southold, Long Island
>   m. Grace Brockett, c. 1684
>   d. August 1 , 1737; Southold, Long Island
>   Children
>>   Mary (see below)
>>   John - b.c. 1690; Southold, Long Island
>>>   m. Hannah Landon; February 25, 1716
>>>   d. March 24, 1768
>>   Josiah - b. 1693; Southold, Long Island
>>>   m. Patience Corwin; February 25, 1724
>>   Daniel - b.c. 1694; Southold, Long Island
>>>   m. Hannah Griffing; October 10, 1717
>>>   d. October 4, 1746; Southold, Long Island
>>   Samuel - b. 1696
>>>   m. Hannah Petty
>>   Benjamin - b. 1706
>>   Abigail
>>   Irene
>>   Tabitha
>>   Obadiah
>>   James

Mary
>   b. betw 1690 and 1696
>   m. James Landon; May, 1707; Southold, Long Island
>   d. August 22, 1722; Southold, Long Island
>   Children

Mary	Joseph	James
Daniel	Rachel	John
David	Lydia	

Charles M. Vail, in <u>Vail and Armstrong</u> mentioned the earliest Vail he found was Geoffrey Le Veel who emigrated with the Normans. His name appeared on the Roll of Battle Abbey. The <u>Genealogical Tables of the Sovereigns of the World</u> by Rev. William Betham, arranged by the Dutchess of Cleveland, and printed by William Bennet of London in 1795, gave a genealogy of Jeremiah Vail that was pretentious to say the least (see Appendix IX). It began at generation one with "Antenor I, King of the Cimmerians; died B.C. 443," and continued through

Charlemagne at generation 49, John La Veyle (King John) at generation 63; to John Veale, who married Alice Moore. John and Alice were the parents of Jeremiah, according to the genealogy. There was no indication on these tables as to the sources of information. While the lineage given was fun, it was also quite dubious. However, it was interesting to note that both Jeremiah and his brother Thomas named sons "John", the name of the man Betham reported was their father.

There has been much discussion as to the origin of the family. While there was some evidence that the family originated in Wales, the vast majority of the Vail family genealogists have supported England as the Vails' homeland. Douglas Campbell, in The Puritans in Holland, England and America, said Salem, where Jeremiah first went, was settled by English from eastern and southern counties. There was a record in Genealogy of Some of the Vails Descended from Jeremiah Vail at Salem, Mass., 1639, of a Jeremiah Vail who was executor for a will for a man from Gloucester, a city on the Severn River, northeast of Bristol, England. Interestingly enough, the 1795 Vail genealogy by Bethan also placed the family in the Gloucester area.

From Moses Vail came the argument that the Veale/Vail names were common in England, but scarcely found in Wales. Although the author suggested the possibility that Gloucestershire on the west coast of England was the home of the Vails, he supported the theory that they originated in Suffolk Co. England, probably from Southwold on the North Sea. The author cited several extracts from the Southwold Parish Register beginning with 1602. Many Veales appeared including frequent references to "Thomas", the name of Jeremiah's brother.

Parish records from Lavenham in Suffolk County, England, also included a number of "Vales" in the 1500's. Simon Aires (Eyre), son of Simon and Susan Vale Aires of Lavenham, emigrated to New England in 1635. John Vale was buried there on February 26, 1565 and another John Vale was married there in 1575.

It might be interesting to note that Thomas Moore of Southold also originated in Southwold, England. And Betham stated that an Alice Moore was the mother of Jeremiah and Thomas Vail.

Jeremiah Vail died in Southold, Suffolk County, Long Island; a settlement begun by Rev. John Youngs, originally from Southwold, England. Had Jeremiah originated in Suffolk County, England, he would have been there at the same time as Rev. Youngs, Thomas Moore, and many others who eventually settled Southold, Long Island.

Whatever his ancestry, Jeremiah Vail was born circa 1618. Although Charles Armstrong claimed Jeremiah emigrated on board the "James" in 1644 from Bristol, Jeremiah first appeared in records dated July 24, 1639, when he was a witness in a court in Salem, Massachusetts. His brother Thomas was also in Salem in the 1640's. Obviously the 1639 record and Armstrong's claim that Jeremiah emigrated in 1644 do not agree. In the 1640's, Salem, with approximately 1000 inhabitants, was the largest English-speaking settlement in America.

On April 6, 1645, Jeremiah's wife Catherine had been admitted to the First Church of Salem. Their daughter Abigail was baptized in that church in 1645, Sarah in 1646/7 and son Jeremiah, Jr. in 1649. As blacksmith, Jeremiah became a proprietor in 1647. In 1648 he bought land in Salem which he sold again in 1651.

On June 17, 1651, Southampton, Long Island granted a 100 pound lot to "Jeremy Veale, Blacksmith of Salem provided he do come and settle here before January next and that his power be in readiness doe all the blacksmith work that the inhabitants doe stand in need of." The offer was probably made at the urging of Thomas Vail, Jeremiah's brother, who had been a Southampton resident since before May 10, 1649.

Jeremiah, however, did not accept the offer. Instead he took charge of the farm of Lt. Lion Gardiner of Gardiner's Island, then named the Isle of Wright. He was in charge of the farm work and clearing new land for cultivation. While on the island, Jeremiah had a difference with an Indian over a canoe. In court the case was decided against Jeremiah and he was ordered to pay damages.

On February 12, 1655, Easthampton gave Jeremiah a lot adjoining Joshua Garlic and opposite the Presbyterian church. Jeremiah and his family lived there from 1655-1659.

During their stay in Easthampton, their neighbor "Goody Garlick was accused of being a witch. While the witchcraft trails of Salem were to become the most famous, the hysteria reached other areas of the New World too. Jeremiah and Catherine Vail appeared as witnesses for Mrs. Garlick in a local hearing. She was then sent to New Haven for trial. There, she was found innocent.

But Mrs. Garlick was one of the lucky ones. Many trials and a number of executions in Connecticut and New Haven took place as early as 1647, even though the infamous Salem Witch Trials would not take place until the 1690's.

By March, 1659, Jeremiah had sold his home and some of his property in Easthampton to Robert Parsons and John Kirkland and had moved to Southold, Long Island. Just before or just after leaving Easthampton, Catherine died. In Southold, he married Mary Folger Paine on May 24, 1660. The couple lived on a lot previously owned by Peter Paine, Mary's first husband. Three children were born to Jeremiah and Mary - John in 1663, Daniel circa 1665, and Mary in 1667.

A letter dated October 4, 1662, and signed by Jeremiah Vail and 31 other residents appointed Col. John Youngs, Jr. as deputy when Southold was given a new charter which put it under the Connecticut Colony jurisdiction.

In 1676, Jeremiah was taxed 152 pounds as one of the more well-to-do in Southold. But by 1683, his taxes had dropped to 74 pounds. It has been suggested he made provisions for his old children before making his will and lowering his taxes. In 1676, Jeremiah had had approximately 500 acres of his own, in addition to 50 acres and a 4-acre homelot originally owned by his second wife, Mary Folger Paine.

Jeremiah was administrator of Nathaniel Pierson, Sr.'s estate in Salem in 1683. On July 18, 1685, Jeremiah signed a deed with his third wife Joyce, his son John, and John's wife

Grace. Jeremiah's second wife Mary had died by that time and Jeremiah had remarried.

In the 1686 census, Jeremiah's family consisted of four males and two females. These probably included Jeremiah, his sons John and Daniel, his third wife Joyce, and his daughter-in-law Grace. The fourth male was unaccounted for, but perhaps it was Jeremy Foster whom Jeremiah provided for in his will.

His will was dated December 4, 1685 in Southold; and probated October 19, 1687. So Jeremiah probably died in 1687 at about 70 years of age. He gave his house, some land, his household goods and animals to his son John. Joyce would maintain "her thirds during her life." He gave other land to his son Daniel; to Jeremy Foster; and to his friend and neighbor, Thomas Tustan.

His daughter Catherine, who was baptized in 1646/7 in Salem, married Nathaniel, son of Thomas and Mary Youngs Moore. She was the mother of Elizabeth.

Jeremiah's son John was born in Southold, Long Island in 1663. After his father's death, John and his family lived in the house he had inherited from his father. In the 1698 census, they were still living there with John's stepmother, Joyce Vail. Circa 1684, John married Grace, probably the daughter of John Brockett who had lived for a while on John Budd's lot.

On November 9, 1864, John was appointed guardian to Jeremiah Foster, a cordwainer from Southampton, who had been named a beneficiary in Jeremiah Vail's will. On December 17, 1694, John and his brother Jeremiah, Jr. made a joint deed for land for a windmill at Orient Point at the tip of Long Island.

John and Grace had ten children - Abigail, Irene, Tabitha, John, Mary, Obadiah, Josiah, Daniel, Samuel and Benjamin. One other possible son was James who died in Albany on September 9, 1745.

Two John Vails were listed on the Southold Militia for 1715 under Capt. Benjamin Youngs. They were probably John, Sr. and John, Jr. of this genealogy. John, Sr. would have been 52 years old and John, Jr. would have been 25.

John Vail, Sr. died August 18, 1737. His daughter Mary was born between 1690 and 1696 in Southold. She married James Landon, a cordwainer, in May, 1707, in Southold and had eight children. She died August 20 or 22, 1722 in Southold and was buried in the church cemetery there.

Chapter 16

Warren Family

Thomas
  b. Southwold, Suffolk Co., England
  d. March, 1641; Southwold, England
  Children
        Mary (see below)
        Elizabeth - m. Thomas Gooch; Southwold, England
        Margaret - m. Capt. Joseph Youngs; February 5, 1632;
              Southwold, England
              Children
                    Joseph
                    John
                    Christopher and/or Thomas, Gideon, Samuel
        Christian - m. Symon Barnard
        Robert - d. by 1641
        Thomas
        George
        Deborah

Mary
    m1. Thomas Gardiner or Gardner
    m2. John Youngs; circa 1639
    will dated November 5, 1678; Southold. Long Island
    Children by Thomas
        Mary - b.c. 1630
              m. John Youngs, Jr.
              d. May 24, 1689
    Children by John
        Benjamin - b.c. 1640; Southold, Long Island
              m. Elizabeth
              d. 169 ; Southold, Long Island
        Christopher - b.c. 164 ; Southold, Long Island
              m1. Mary
              m2. Mary or Marie, dau of John Budd; c. 1675;
              Southold, Long Island
              d. July 31, 1695; Southold, Long Island

Men hired by William the Conquerer to guard forests against
poachers were called "foresters" or "warrenders". Their
authority was nearly absolute. In later years, after watchmen
became known as "warrens", the title became part of the
watchman's name.

Others with that surname were descended from Anglo-Norman
families from the hamlet of Varenne in Normandy, France, and
adopted variations of the town's name for their own.

Years later, the Thomas Warren (Warryn) of this genealogy
was a wealthy merchant in Southwold, Suffolk County, England. In
his will, Thomas left his son Thomas, Jr. his primary house and
lands (see Appendix X). He made bequests to only two
grandchildren - Mary "Gardiner" received thirty pounds and
Benjamin Youngs received ten pounds. Their mother, Thomas'
daughter, received nothing. And her son Christopher had not yet
been born. Thomas bequeathed thirty pounds to his daughter
Margaret, wife of Joseph Youngs, but did not mention her already
born children, John and Joseph.

Sisters Margaret and Mary Warren married brothers and
emigrated to the New World. Margaret married Captain Joseph

Youngs before emigrating. Mary married, first, Thomas Gardiner (Gardner) in England and, second, Rev. John Youngs after arriving in the New World.

Chapter 17

Youngs Family

Rev. Christopher
    m. Margaret (d. October 27, 1630; buried November 5, 1630,
    Southwold, England)
    d. June 14, 1626; Southwold, Suffolk Co., England
    Children
        John (see below)
        Mary - b.c. 1609; Southwold, England
            m. William, son of Francis Browne
            d. 1637; Salem, Massachusetts
        Martha - m. Thomas Moore; by July, 1636
        Joseph - m. Margaret Warren; February 5, 1632;
            Southwold, England
            d.c. 1669; Southold, Long Island
            Children
                Joseph - bapt. June 23, 1633; Southwold,
                    England
                    m. Elizabeth
                    d. aft January, 1706; Southold, Long
                    Island
                    Children
                        Joseph - b. Southold, Long Island
                        Josiah - b. Southold, Long Island
                            m1. Mary by 1698
                            m2. Experience Landon
                            d. 1732; Aqueboque, Long
                            Island
                            Children
                              Bethia - m. Noah Hallock
                      Thomas - b. Southold, Long Island
                          m. Elizabeth
                        d.c. 1750; Oyster Bay, Long
                        Island
                      Mary - b. Southold, Long Island
                John - bapt. March 10, 1635
                Christopher and/or Thomas, Gideon, Samuel
        Christopher II - m. Priscilla, dau of Richard Elvin
            d. 1647; Wenham, Massachusetts
            will dated April 19, 1647
            Children
                 Sarah - b. October, 1639
                 Mary - b. 1642
                 Christopher - b. July, 1642
                      d. November, 1643
                 Christopher - December 2, 1644
        Elizabeth - d. young
        Margaret
        Edward (?)

Rev. John
    b. 1598; England
    m1. Joan Herrington (d. 1630, England); Southwold, England
    m2. Joan Harris, wid of Richard Palgrave; 1630
    m3. Mary, wid of Thomas Gardner, dau of Thomas Warren; c.
    1639; Salem, Massachusetts
    d. February 24, 1672; Southold, Long Island
    Children by Joan Herrington
        John - bapt. April 10, 1623; Southwold, England
            m1. Mary, dau of Thomas and Mary Gardner
            m2. Hannah or Anne Tooker

```
                d. April 18, 1698; Southold, Long Island
                Children
                        Thomas - m. Mary
                        Zerubbable
        Thomas - b. May 1, 1625; Southwold, England
                m1. Rebecca, dau of Thomas Mapes
                m2. Sarah, dau of John Frost; 1658
        Children by Joan Harris Palgrave
                Mary - b. 1633; Southwold, England
                        m. Edward Petty; by 1658; Southold, Long Island
                        Children
                                John - b. November 26, 1658
                                        m. Mary Charfield
                                Edward - b. November 26, 1658
                                James - b. 1663
                                Joseph - m. Mary Salmon
        Children by Mary Warren Gardiner
                Christopher III (see below)
                Benjamin - b.c. 1640
                        m. Elizabeth
                        d. 1697; Southold, Long Island
                        Children
                                John - b.c. 1676
                                Benjamin - m. Mercy Landon
                                Eliza - m. Stephen "Swzey"
                                Christian - m1. William Horton; December 31,
                                        1702
                                        m2. David Youngs; June, 1709
        Mother Unknown
                Rachel - b. Southwold, England
                Joseph - b. Southwold, England
                        m. Sara, sis of Barnabas Wines


Christopher III
        b.c. 1642; Southold, Long Island
        m2. Mary (Marie), dau of John Budd; c. 1675; Southold, Long
        Island
        d. July 31, 1695; Southold, Long Island
        Children
                Christopher IV (see below)
                Benjamin - b. 1668
                        m. Mary Grover or Glover
                        d. August, 1742
                        Children
                                Benjamin - b. March 27, 1703
                                        d. September 26, 1729
                                Deborah - b. February 14, 1704/5; Southold,
                                        Long Island
                                        m. Capt. John Ledyard, c. 1727
                                        d. March 18, 1746/7
                                daughter - m. Robert Hempsted
                                daughter - m. Ebenezer Prime
                John - b. October or November 21, 1679; Southold, Long
                        Island
                        m1. Ann Hallock; January 7, 1707
                        m2. Sarah Terry; November 6, 1745
                        m3. Elizabeth Gardner; November 30, 1745
                        d. March 3, 1750; Aqueboque, Long Island
                        Children
                                Isiah - b. 1717
                                        d. 1729
                                David - b. January, 1720
```

                    m. Bethia Parshall
                    d. April 18, 1752; Brookhaven, Long
                    Island
          Anne - b. 1683; Southold, Long Island
                    m. Richard Brown; February 21, 1705; Southold,
                    Long Island
                    d. November 23, 1748; Southold, Long Island
                    Children
                         Anne   Henry   Richard
                         Christopher   Mehetable   Peter
                         Dorothy
          Phebe - b.c. 1690
                    m. Henry Tuthill, Jr.; December 10, 1717
                    d. September 1, 1775
                    Children
                         Azariah   Christopher   Phebe
                         Perh Mehetable Nathaniel   Bethia
                         Zipporah
          Sarah (?)

Christopher IV
     b. 1675; Southold, Long Island
     m. Elizabeth (1679-1717/18), dau of Nathaniel Moore; c.
     1697; Southold, Long Island
     d. June 28, 1729; Aqueboque, Long Island
     Children
          Martha (see below)
          Christopher V - b. 1700
                    m. Joanna Parshall
          Daniel - b. 1712; Aqueboque, Long Island
                    m. Mary Penny; October 10, 1732
                    d. January 18, 1755; Aqueboque, Long Island
                    will probated February 6, 1755

Martha
     b. aft 1697
     m. Daniel Landon; May 22, 1736
     d. September 20, 1800
     Children
          Daniel   Abner   Molly
          John   Seth   Nathan
          Oliver   Joseph

     The name has been found as Young, Yong, Yonge and Youngs.
For the purpose of this genealogy, the spelling will be
"Youngs". In Our Young Family in America, Prof. Edward Hudson
Young wrote that "Young" was the spelling of his New Jersey
ancestors who were Quakers from Scotland. He also claimed that
"Yong was phonetic and bad spelling rather than a variant of the
English Yonge." Selah Youngs, author of Youngs Family believed
the Long Island branch of the family originated in Wales. As an
argument, he cited the fact the coat of arms for Tudor Treavor
of Wales appeared on the 1697 will of John Youngs, Jr. Selah
Youngs also noted there were Youngs among the descendents of
Tudor Treavor.

     Christopher Youngs I may have been born as early as 1545.
Selah Youngs suggested that Christopher was the son of
Christopher Younge, Vicar of Ashburton and Ermington. In 1633,
Robert Gill of Paulton, England, was the father-in-law of Henry
Yonge of "Brynyorkin" who was a relative of Christopher of
Ashburton. In 1640, John Young, son of Christopher I of
Southwold, had an apprentice name Robert Gell. Selah proposed

it that "this boy (Robert Gell) belonged to the Gill family of Paulton, and that when Captain Joseph Youngs made a voyage to England in 1638, he visited his relatives there, and on his return young Robert Gell came with him to America."

If Christopher was really born in 1545; he began college, married Margaret and began a family late in life. There were two possible reasons for this "late start". Queen Elizabeth I did not approve of priests marrying and that may have forced him to wait. However, since John was born in 1598, Christopher was married before Queen Elizabeth's death. And Christopher was not ordained until 1600, or age 55 if he was indeed born in 1545.

Another possible reason for Christopher's late marriage to Margaret was that she was Christopher's second wife. In Immigrants to the Middle Colonies, Christopher was listed as having married a young widow named Levington or Levingston. It also stated that her daughter by her first husband was Ann Palgrave who, it continued, went to the New World. But Christopher I never went to the New World and could not have been an immigrant to a middle colony. However, his son Christopher, Jr. did emigrate. And his son John married Joan, the widow of Richard Palgrave. When John requested emigration to America in 1637, he listed, in addition to his own children, another child named Anne. That child was probably Anne Palgrave, daughter of Joan.

If Christopher's birthdate was correct, he was 53 when his son John was born in 1598. Mary was born in 1609, when Christopher was 64. Other children included Martha, Joseph, Christopher II, Elizabeth and Margaret. If there was another son named Edward as sometimes reported, he had died by 1626, when his father's will was written.

Christopher had entered at Cambridge University circa 1593. He was on a list of all students at Cambridge and received a scholarship on April 25, 1593. He was granted a B.A. in 1596 and a M.A. in 1600. Christopher was ordained as deacon in Norwich on December 21, 1599 and as priest on April 25, 1600. Perhaps he remained in Norwich until moving to Southwold.

Southwold, in England's easternmost county of Suffolk, is two km southeast of Reydon and twenty miles south of Yarmouth. Once an important North Sea fishing port, changes in the harbor greatly handicaped Southwold's economic development. Southwold means "south woodlands" in Old English.

John Browne's history of Congregationalism in Suffolk Co. reported that Southwold was begun as a chapelry connected with Reydon. According to Genealogical Gleanings in England, "A mandate was issued March, 1611, for inducing Christopher Yonges, clerk, into the real possessions of the vicarage of Reydon." Parish records indicated that on January 14, 1611, "Christopher Yong was inducted into the living of Reydon and Southwold" and served as the vicar of St. Margarets from 1611 to 1626. The church was referred to in the Doomsday Book as early as 1081-1086 as "St. Margarits, Ressenure" (Reydon).

Margery Smith's 1624 will mentioned Christopher as a clerk in Southwold, England. Robert Page of Southwold willed Rev. Christopher Youngs five shillings in February, 1617, and Robert Williamson willed him ten shillings on October 25, 1617.

Sometime between 1613 and 1626, Elizabeth Youngs, daughter of Christopher and Margaret, drowned. A large group from Southwold were returning by boat from the Dunwich Fair on St. James Day. When the boat was pulled to shore, it broke lose and the force of the tide carried the boat against the cable and overwhelmed it. Twenty people in addition to Elizabeth Youngs perished. It must have been a very difficult time for the Youngs family. In addition to losing a daughter, Christopher must have lost many parishioners.

Christopher Youngs died June 14, 1626 and was buried two days later in the Southwold church. His will was proven July 5, 1626. He left his wife Margaret all his lands for the rest of her life and named her as executor. He named six living children - John, Joseph, Christopher, Mary, Margaret and Martha - and two grandchildren - John and Thomas Youngs, sons of John (see Appendix XI). Margaret died October 27, 1630 and her will was proven on January 8, 1631.

The History of Congregationalism and Memorials of the Churches in Norfolk and Suffolk related that Christopher was succeeded in the church at Southwold by Rev. Stephen Fen. After Fen's death the town went without a minister for a number of years because the parishioners could not afford to pay the seventy pounds a year needed to support the church and minister.

Christopher and Margaret's children proved to be an adventurous group. John's family emigrated to Salem, Massachusetts in 1637 and later moved to Southold, Long Island. He is discussed more fully later.

Captain Joseph Youngs, master of the "Love", and Margaret Warren (Warryn), daughter of Thomas, were married in Southwold, England. Joseph's son Joseph was baptized at Southwold on January 23, 1633/4 and his son John was baptized there March 23, 1635. Joseph's family followed his brother John to Salem and Southold, Long Island in 1649. At that time, Joseph was captain of the "Mary and Margaret" and made frequent voyages to Barbadoes. In 1652, "Mr. Joseph Yonge of Longe Island" was listed as owing money to the estate of Captain "Bozone" Allen of Suffolk Co., Massachusetts. However, Joseph died in 1657/8 as probably the richest man in Southold, Long Island.

Mary Youngs married merchant William Browne, son of Francis of Wybred Hall. They sailed to Salem and Southold, Long Island, leaving England in July, 1635 aboard Capt. Joseph Young's ship, the "Love".

Christopher Youngs, Jr. and his wife Priscilla may have traveled aboard the same ship. Christopher, Jr.'s will was proven in Wenham, Massachusetts, on June 9, 1647. In his will he directed that his three children be returned to England upon his death. However, the court of Massachusetts ruled otherwise as far as his son was concerned and awarded guardianship to John Phillips of Wenham. The two daughters were put under the guardianship of Christopher II's father-in-law, Richard Elvin, and Christopher's widow, Priscilla of Great Yarmouth, Norfolk, England. Esdras Reed of Wenham, William Brown of Salem, and Mrs. Joseph (Margaret Warren) Youngs were named executors of Christopher's estate.

Christopher, Sr.'s daughter Martha married Thomas Moore, discussed elsewhere. They left England circa 1635 also, and may have traveled to Salem aboard the "Love". They settled for a time in Salem, but eventually moved to Southold, Long Island. Thomas was in Southold in 1651 and Martha, along with their eight children, followed the next year.

According to Planters of the Commonwealth, the voyage to the New World cost an adult pilgrim ten pounds and each had to furnish "their own subsistence." Prices were fixed by the Massachusetts Bay Company and adopted by subsequent ships. For families, costs were "sucking children not to bee reckoned: such as under 4 yeares of age, 3 for one (fare); under 8, 2 for one; under 12, 3 for 2." The cost of shipping household items were an additional "4li. a tonn for goods." Since the average voyage was 5-12 weeks long depending upon the weather, winds, and time of year; a good amount of freight was needed simply for subsistence during the trip. An average family with one ton of freight had to pay a great deal for passage on a damp, cold, overcrowded ship. In This New Man, the American, Miller wrote that the Massachusetts Bay Co. required immigrants to take adequate supplies of food, leather, nails, glass, iron, guns and ammunition, farming implements, household utensils and farm animals. Miller wrote, "Poor Puritans were warned that they could not make it on piety alone."

On July 23, 1622, John married Joan Herrington in Southwold, England, where his father was vicar. Their sons John and Thomas were born in Southwold in 1623 and 1625. respectively. Both boys were baptized in 1625.

The next year John's father died and he inherited all his father's books, except for some in English which his mother, brothers and sisters inherited. John's sons John and Thomas each inherited a silver spoon from their grandfather. Selah Youngs suggested John might have become the minister of St. Margaret's after his father's death.

John's first wife died in 1630, leaving him with at least two small sons. That year he married for a second time. His new wife was Joan Harris; the widow of Richard Palgrave of Great Yarmouth, Norfolk County, and son of John Palgrave of Pulham St. Mary the Virgin. Richard had married Joan in 1625/6 but died shortly after leaving a daughter Anne.

More children were born to John and Joan Harris Palgrave. Mary was born in 1633. Rachel and Joseph were born to one of the Joans.

However, all five children were born by May 11, 1637 when, according to List of Emigrants to America 1600-1700, "John Yonge of St. Margarets, Suff. (35) minister & wife Joan (34) & 6 children - John, Tho. Anne, Rachell, Marey, Josueph" requested to go to Salem, but were forbidden passage from Yarmouth. The Anne listed was probably Anne Palgrave, Joan's daughter by her first marriage. Anne was baptized in Yarmouth. She later married Nicholas Woodbury. Note the age listed for John was 35 in 1637. However, he was more likely 39 years old.

Selah Youngs suggested that John left for New England on the original ship for which he was denied passage. Whether he took the same ship or not, on August 14, 1637, just three months after being denied passage, John and his family had emigrated to Salem.

Salem (Naumkeag) had been settled circa 1623-162 by settlers who survived the break up of the trading post at Cape Anne. The town was formally founded in 1628 by John Endicott. Puritans who arrived in Salem in 1629 were "hard-liners". Old Salem residents who refused to move so far from the Anglican Church doctrine were persecuted as "libertines" and deported. On June 12, 1630, eleven ships of newcomers arrived in Salem, but soon left because the land appeared so desolate. However, between 1628 and 1656, five new towns sprung up from the area originally known as Salem. They were Salem Village. Beverly, Enon (Wenham), Manchester and Marblehead.

John was admitted to Salem on December 25, 1637 and was given a one-acre meadow lot. Three years later, perhaps at the suggestion of Hugh Peters, the former minister, John filled the office of pastor in the church at Salem. John, like his father, had attended Cambridge after receiving a scholarship. He was awarded his B.A. from St. Catherine's in 1623 and later may have become minister at St. Margaret's, Suffolk County. On December 21, 1639, Rev. John was granted fifty additional acres in Salem.

Sometime circa 1639, his second wife died and John took Mary Warren Gardner, widow of Thomas Gardiner, as his third wife. Mary's father had been a merchant in John's hometown in England.

While minister at Salem, John gathered together a small company which settled in an area on Long Island Sound. Originally called Yennycock, the area was later named Southold after John's English home. The colony, settled in September or October, 1640, was on the northeast arm of Long Island. Until 1649, the land was titled to the New Haven Colony.

John was chosen pastor and given the largest homelot and a large division of lands (see Appendix XI). The homelot with adjoining meadowlands faced onto Main Street. He had given all those lands to his sons by his death.

His sons by Mary were probably both born in Southold, Long Island - Benjamin in 1640 and Christopher III in 1642. Christopher III was born the same year the English Civil War began and all theaters in England were closed by order of the Puritans. Benjamin would later become judge of the Suffolk Court of Common Pleas.

In The New Haven Colony, 1658 was given as the year that John Budd was fined for letting Quakers assemble in his home; and Humphrey Norton, a Quaker, was "accused of traducing Rev. John Young...and reviling magistrates and government" in Southold's meeting house. At his March 1 , 1658 trial Norton was not allowed to answer the accusations. As punishment, he was whipped, branded with "H" for "heretic" and fined ten pounds. Since he could not pay the fine, Norton was sentenced to 21 days in a cold open prison with no fire. After two days in irons, a baker from New Amsterdam paid the fine. Norton was banished. Isn't it ironic that the John Young family that immigrated to Morris Co., New Jersey, were Quakers?

Another litigation occurred when John Booth petitioned the council because his goods had been seized for taxes for the minister's salary. Booth had not paid because the minister had refused to baptize his children. The governor and council would not interfere, but recommended the minister show more charity.

Since Rev. John was still living at the time, he was probably the minister involved.

Rev. Youngs died on February 24, 1672 at the age of 74. Barnabas Horton and Barnabas Wines witnessed his death bed oral will making his third wife Mary the executor (see Appendix XI). Mary died in Southold in 1678. Both were buried in the cemetery of the First Presbyterian Church of Southold founded in 1640 by Rev. John Youngs.

His daughter Mary had married Edward Petty, a ship's carpenter, by 1658. She probably had died by May 15, 1671, when Edward Petty gave their two youngest children, James and Joseph, to Thomas and Nathaniel Moore to raise. Thomas and Nathaniel were related to Mary. After 1671, Edward married for a second time.

John Youngs, Jr. was nearly as famous in Southold as his father. In 1653 he married Mary Gardner, daughter of his father's third wife. About that time, Cromwell was at war with Holland and was attempting to influence the New England Colonies to capture New York from the Dutch. John, Jr. visited several Connecticut towns trying to raise a force to drive the Dutch out of Amsterdam. As a result, he was in direct conflict with Southold and New Haven policies. So John joined forces with Capt. John Scott, who had made a fortune as a buccaneer, to work at preventing Indian interference in the Anglo-Dutch War. From 1654-1656, John Youngs, Jr. commanded a patrol boat on Long Island Sound to prevent Indian attacks. During that time he was arrested by New Amsterdam officials for privateering and imprisoned on the "King Solomon". By the time a bond was posted, John, Jr. had already escaped. When he discovered his bail had been paid, Youngs returned to the Dutch and was released. In May, 1654, he was tried in New Haven, admitted guilt and was fined one hundred pounds.

In 1660, John, Jr. was appointed magistrate and deputy from Southold for the New Haven Colony. However, he favored a Long Island-Connecticut union and, on October 19, 1662, he proclaimed all Long Island towns were under Connecticut jurisdiction. According to A Sweet and Alien Land, Youngs had delivered letters to English towns under Dutch rule - Gravesend, Newton, Hempstead and Flushing - stating "whereas it hath pleased his Majesty to involve Long Island within Connecticut Patten: by virtue where of the General Assembly at Hartford have ordered me to give notice to every Town upon Long Island, that they are under the Jurisdiction of Connecticut."

The Dutch protested. So in 1663, John Young, Jr. commanded the Southold militia and horse troop in an attack of Flushing. On May 12, 1664, he joined Winthrop's Council and, that summer, aided in the capture of New Amsterdam.

On October 31, 1676, Southold accepted a patent from the Duke of York. John Youngs, Jr. and six others were patentees. In 1681, he drew up a petition for a representative assembly in the colony and served as high sheriff. He was lieutenant-colonel of the horse troops in Southold in 1687 and colonel of the Suffolk County militia in 1689. He served for twelve years on various governor's councils. John Youngs, Jr, died April 12, 1698.

His brother Benjamin was elected Recorder in Southold in 1674 and was re-elected yearly until his death in 1697. He was one of six patentees along with his half-brother John Youngs, Jr., Joshua Horton, Barnabas Horton, Samuel Glover and Jacob Corey. When Gov. Andrus signed the October 31, 1676 patent for Southold, Benjamin and his wife Elizabeth were living in the homestead he had inherited from his mother. In 1675 he was on the tax list with a worth of 142 pounds. In 1694 he indentured his son Benjamin to learn the weaver's trade from John Alaban.

Rev. John Young's sons Christopher III and Thomas left Southold and settled in Elizabethtown, New Jersey. But in November, 1667 Christopher sold his house and lands in Elizabethtown.

By 1668 he was settled back in Southold and was married to a woman named Mary. Benjamin was probably a child of that marriage. Mary died young and Christopher married Mary or Marie, daughter of John Budd, in 1675. At the time he was a landowner and mariner owning half-interest in the "Speedwell". Although he was worth 120.1 pounds, by 1683 he was worth only 80 pounds. Christopher III and Marie had Christopher IV in 1675, John in 1679, and Anne in 1683.

The 1686 census showed Christopher III had four males, two females and no slaves living in his home. The two females were Marie and Anne. The four males would have been Christopher III, Christopher IV, Benjamin, and John.

Christopher III died July 31, 1695 leaving no will. His wife Mary and eldest son Benjamin were appointed joint administrators.

Christopher IV was married in Southold circa 1697 to Elizabeth Moore, daughter of Nathaniel. In the 1698 census, they were living with his mother Marie.

In 1712 Christopher IV and his brother John were living on a farm at Aqueboque which their mother Marie had inherited from Lt. John Budd. John Young's land ran north from Queens Road to the sound, with the exception of a "strip two rods wide on the east" which went to Christopher. Land on the south side of Queens Road extending to the bay also went to Christopher. In 1704, Christopher bought the original Thomas Moore homelot on the south side of Town Street.

While Christopher IV was primarily a landowner/farmer, he also was active in the local military. In 1715 he was in the Southold Horse Troop under Captain John Cooper. He died on September 1, 1727. The inventory taken afterwards listed 30 head of cattle, 45 sheep and 4 horses. The New York Inventory of Wills, Book I, pages 128-129 showed the dispensation of his estate. His son Christopher V was appointed administrator on December 20, 1728.

Christopher V was also administrator of his mother's 1717/8 will and of his brother Daniel's 1755 will. Both Daniel and Christopher V were listed as residents of Southold in the New York Court of Appeals papers concerning Daniel's will.

Christopher IV's daughter Martha married Daniel Landon, son of James, on May 22, 1736, the year Patrick Henry was born. In

1740 they moved to Litchfield, Connecticut, where they joined
the Anglican Church.

Loyalists were probably strongest in New York. In fact,
according to <u>The Price of Loyalty</u>, in January, 1775, the New
York Assembly was "dominated by open loyalists" who "refused to
appoint delegates to the Second Continental Congress." But the
people of Southold strongly supported independence. Daniel and
Martha, however, supported the British during the American
Revolution and suffered a great deal during those times. Several
of their children settled in Canada as a result. Daniel and
Martha, however, stayed in Litchfield and Martha Youngs Landon
died there on September 20, 1800.

THE VISITATION OF SUFFOLK, 1561

Arms:

Quarterly: 1 & 4,BROCKETT.2,FITZSYMON.3,?Broket [Or on a pile
Azure a griffin passant Arent}.[The martlet for difference]

I.   JOHN BROCKETT. Of Brockett Hall and Wheathampstead, co.
     Herts. Married Dorothy, daughter of ___ Hewson (A).
     Issue:

     1.   SIR JOHN. Of Brockett Hall. Dubbed a 'Knighte of the
          Carpett' by Edward VI., 22 February 1546 (Metcalfe.
          Knights. 92). Marriage and issue (A)
     2.   NICHOLAS. Of Markeatsell [sic], co. Herts. Marriage
          and issue (A)
     3.   EDWARD.
     4.   ROBERT. II.
     5.   JANE. Married William Copwood, of Totteridge, co.
          Herts [see Copwood Pedigree, Visitation of
          Hertfordshire 1572
          (ed. Metcalfe) 6]
     6.   LUCY. Married Thomas Hoo, of Paul's Walden, co. Herts
          [see Hoo Pedigrees, Visitations of Hertfordshire 1572
          & 1634 (ed. Metcalfe) 12-13, 65]

II. ROBERT BROCKETT. Of Westleton and Bramfield. Subsidy Return
     1568, Bramfield. Robert Brocket gent _5 in goodes' (S.G.B.
     XII. 51). Burial, Bramfield. 1582.'May 18. Roberd Brockket,
     ge' (B.75). Will dated 24 November 1580, proved at
     Halesworth
     7 August 1582. To be buried in Bramfield churchyard;
     'Margarett my wiff; my sonnes Raynold brokket, willm
     brokett, John brokett; my daughters slys brockett, Margaret
     brokett, Dorothe brokett, Elynore brokett, Anne brokett'.
     All children under twenty-four. Wife sole executrix;
     'Raynold Rabett and Robt ffarrer' both of Bramfield,
     supervisors. Lands, etc., in Walpole and Cookley (Ips.
     Rec. Off. C. inv.,fo.99) Married, 1st., after 1547/8,
     Margaret, daughter of William Gilbert, Clothier, or Clare;
     whose will dated 1547/8 (Thornton. History of Clare. 185;
     Thompson.Family and Arms of Gilbert of Colchester. 198,
     ped.) Marriage, Bramfield. 1557. 'May 3. Robart Brockett
     and Margaret ffarro' (B.51). Margaret, stated to be
     daughter of Henry Farrar, of Bramfield. A few months
     after Brockett's death, and pregnant by his, she married
     William Dowty or Daughty. Issue [by first wife]:

     1.   [ELIZABETH]. Baptism, Bramfield. 1554. ¨June 19.
          Elizabeth Brockett dowghter of Robart Brockett and
          Margaret his wyf' (B.5). Dead before 1561.
     2.   [DOROTHY, the elder]. Baptism, Bramfield. 1557.
          'Feb. 14. Dorythie Brokett dowghter of Rob't
          Brockett and m'garet his wyff' (B.5). Dead before
          1561.
     3.   ALICE. [By father's second wife]. In father'
          will, 1580.
     4.   THOMAS. Baptism, Bramfield. 1569. 'May 8. Thommes
          Broccket sonne vnto Robert Broccket gen' and
          Margaret his wyfe' (B.7). In father's will.
          Baptism, Bramfield. 1571. 'Oct.

5. JOHN   John Broccket and Elyne Broccket
6. ELEANOR   sonne and daughter vnto Robert
Broccket and Margaret his wif'
(B.7). Both in father's will.

7. ROSE. Baptism, Bramfield. 1575. 'Feb. 12. Rose
Brokket daughter vnto Roberd broccket ge' and
Margaret his wif' (B.8). Burial, Bramfield. 1575.
'May 6. Rose Brocket d. vnto Mr. Brocket, gen.,
and Margaret his wyfe' (B.75)

8. ANNE. Baptism, Bramfield. 1578.'Dec. 21. Ane
Brocket dawter vnto Roberd Brockkett ge' and his
wif' (B.8). In father's will.

9. REGINALD.
10. WILLIAM.   In father's will.
11. MARGARET.
12. DOROTHY, the younger.
13. ROBERT. Baptism, Bramfield. 1582 [sic]. 'Jan. 13.
Roberd Brockket sonne of Roberd Brockket ge' and
Margerit his wif. Now allso ye soone of Will'm
Dowtye who married the wif of ye forsayd Roberd
Brocket after she was conceyuyd wt this child av
monthes as by this Register it doo apear both of
the deth of ye forsayd Roberd Brockket & allso of
ye marrige of the sayd Will'm Dowtye vnto ye wif
of ye forsayd Will'm' [sic]. (B.(). [The marriage
of Margaret and Dowty does not appear in the
Register and, as Brocket was not buried until 18
May 1582, this baptism must have been in 1583]

Sources:
A. Brockett Pedigree. Visitation of Hertfordshire 1634.(H.S.)
p.32.
B. Hill. Registers of the Parish of Bramfield.

See also:
Brockett Pedigree. Visitation of Essex 1558. (H.S.) p.30

From tomb of Lion Gardiner:

In Memory of Lion Gardiner

An officer of ye English Army and An Engineer Mafter of
Workes of Fortifications in ye Leaguers of ye Prince of Orange
in ye Low Countries - In 1635 he came to New England

In ye Service of a Company of Lords & Gentlemen he bvilded
& Commanded ye Saybrook Forte

After completing this term of service he removed in 1639 to
his
land of which he was fole owner & P.vire. Born in 1599 he died
in
this Towne in 1663 Venerated and honoured.

Under many trying Circumftances in Peace and War he was
Brave discreet & Trve.

Inscription on the four sides of a large tomb with a recumbent
figure of a man in armor on it.

From **Pequot Warres** by Lion Gardiner

    "In the year 1635, I Lion Gardiner, Engineer and Master of
works of Fortification in the legers of the Prince of Orange, in
the Low Countries, through the persuasion of Mr John Davenport,
Mr Hugh Peters with some other well-affected Englishmen of
Rotterdam, I made an agreement with the forenamed Mr Peters for
100 pounds per annum, for four years to serve the company of
patentees, namely, the Lord Say, and the Lord Brooks [Brook],
Sir Arthur Hazilrig, Sir Mathew Bonnington [Bonighton?], Sir
Richard Saltingstone [Saltonstall], Esquire Fenwick, and the
rest of their company, [I say] I was to serve them only in the
drawing, ordering and making of a city, town, or forts of
defence... Mr Winthrop, Mr Fenwick and Mr Peters persuaded me
that they would do their utmost endeavour to persuade the Bay-
men to desist from war a year or two, till we could be better
provided for it...
    So they returned to Boston. But our great ____tation [of
having many laborers sent to him] at the River's mouth, came
only to two men, viz. Mr Fenwick and his man, who came with Mr
Hugh Peters, and Mr Oldham and Thomas Stanton, bringing with
them some Otter-skin coats, and Beaver and skeins of wampum."

Mass. Hist. Coll., 3rd series, Vol. III, p. 136.

Richard, Seigneur de Loudun   Guillaume, Seigneur du
   b. France   Tronchet au Maine
   m. Isabeau de Gemages   m. P h i l i p p i n e
   Children   d'Antoigne
        Alix (see below)   d. November 10, 1305
                                          Children
                                               Geoffroy (see
                                                  below)
                                               Jean - m. Jeanne du
                                                  Fay
                                               Huet
                                               Herbert - religious
                                                  career at
                                                  Couture du
                                                  Mans

Alix de Loudun   married in 1298   Geoffroy Morin, Seigneur
   b. France   du Tronchet au Maine
   d. 1339   d. 1355

          Children of Alix and Geoffroy
               Guillaume (see below)
               Roger - still living 1379

     Since Guillaume II was the eldest son of Geoffroy Morin,
Seigneur du Tronchet au Maine and Alix, the only child of
Richard, Seigneur de Loudun; he inherited both titles

          Guillaume II, Seigneur de Loudun et du Tronchet
               m. Jeanne Pezas (d. by 1388)
               d. May 24, 1364 in the Battle of Cocherel
               Children
                    Guillaume III (see below)

          Guillaume III, Seigneur de Loudun et du Tronchet
               m. Marie de Dreax (d. April 18, 1413), dau of
               Etienne de Dreux and Marguerite de Boulainvillers
               (1st wife) or Phillippe de
               Muffigny (2nd wife). A descendent of Lois le
               Gros, Roi de France (1081-113)
               d. by 1416, Loudun au Maine
               Children
                    Jean (see below)
                    Guillaume - d. 1415 in Battle of Azincourt
                    Geoffroy - m. Guyonne Ainous de Montibaut
                    (d. 1464)
                         d. 1421 in Battle of Veineuil
                         Children
                              Catherine - d. 1451
                    Pierre
                    Jean le Jeune - formed Seigneur de
                         Banneviller branch
                    12 Other Children

          Jean, Seigneur de Loudun et du Tronchet (Titled in
          1451 after the death of his two older brothers and his
          niece)
               m. Marie du Gueschlin, wid of Michael le Roy,
               Seigneur de Verrouliere-en-Chateauneuf; dau of
               Guillaume, Seigneur de la Roberie and Fleurie

```
Morin
Children
        Jacques (see below)
        Guillaume IV, Seigneur de Loudun et du
        Tronchet
                m. Jeanne de Thavalle (d. 1513), 1469
                d. 1501

    Jacques de Loudun
        b. France
        Children
                Jacques (see below)
                Pierre Charles

Jacques de Loudun
        b. France
        m. Mlle Le Duc, 1550, England
        r. England aft 1550
        Children
                Georges (see Landon Family)
                Nathaniel
                Jacques
```

Coat of Arms

Lordships of Landon, of Beaumont, of Youerse of Champs Maria, of La Carston, of Tronchet.

Of blue, with 3 cocks of gold posed two above and one below, the beaks, crests and claws of red, right foot drawn up.

Supports: Two savage gentlemen of a pink color, with girdle and coronet or ivy and leaning on rough or natural wood clubs. Supporters are distinctive of high rank and usually only used by sovereigns or peers of the realm. It is improper for any American to use them as it denotes he has been given the right by special grant.

Helmet: That of Chevaliers or Lords

Motto: "We Fight Valiantly". The motto was originally a word or sentence which formed a war cry. The motto may be older then the Coat of Arms.

Abstract from Southold Town Records

I Thomas Moor Senr of Southold doe give grant and make over all my housing, lands and cattle, horse kinde, Swine & Sheepe and Sloope, with all my moveables within doors and without, to my son Nathaniel More he allowing his father and mother sufficient maintenance during their lives.

Witness my hand and seale.
Witness   EDWARD PATTY
           SAMUEL SMYTH   THOMAS MOOR

Acknowledged 7 March 1680 before me
                              JOHN YONGS, Sherife-

The above written deed made void 30 June 1691.

Entd 1689/90, 6 Mar
     Pr Benj Yo. Rdr.

Will of Thomas Moore

In ye name of God Amen - I Thomas Moore of Southold in ye County of Suffolk on Long Island in ye Province of N. Yorke being Exercized under the afflicting hand of God with great weakness yet of sound memory do make constitute & ordain this writing to be my last Will & Testamt. first I bequeath my soul into ye hands of God who gave it and my body being dead to be decently buried in hopes of its resurrection at ye last day unto Eternal life & as for my worldly estate my debts & funeral charges being first paid I do order give dispose & bequeath in manner & form foll.
Impmis. I do give & bequeath unto my wife Catherine Moore one third of all my goods land commonages & meadow lands dwelling houses barns orchards garden fences & fencing stuffe corn cattle horse kind sheep swine household goods of whatsoever sorts that are now belonging & appertaining unto me within the whole town bounds of Southold & every part & parcel of sd goods land estate above mentioned to have & hold to her my said wife Katharine Moore with all the issues profits whatsoever during her widowhood or natural life if she marry not & not be fully freely enjoyed by her.
Item - I give & bequeath unto my eldest son Thomas Moore all my lands together with ye appurtances lying & being in Westhold [sic] near ye fresh pond by ye wading river -
Item - I do give & bequeath unto my third son Nathaniell Moore all my lands & meadows allotments of lands right of lands commonages meadow lands dwelling houses building barns orchards gardens fencing stuffe fencing within the old bounds of ye town that is to say between Wm Wells & Toms Creek head.
Item - I give & bequeath unto my daughters namely Martha Symons Hannah Symons Elizabeth Grover & Sarah Glover all my household goods of whatsoever sort equally to be divided amonst them -

Also my Will is that all the lands estate that are or is herein given to my said sons they shall have hold & enjoy to them their heirs & assigns forever -

Lastly - My Will is that my beloved sons Thomas Moore & Nathaniell Moore shall be the only Executors of this my last Will & Testamt. dated at Southold this 23d of June in ye 3d year of ye reigne of our sovereigne Lonrd Willm ye 3d King of England & defender of ye faith &c. Anno Dom. 1691 -

THOMAS MOORE

Signed sealed & delivered before us
    JOSEPH YOUNG
    BENJN YOUNG

Inventory of Peter Paine's Estate

September 15th 1658
An Inventorie of the 'state of Peter Payne late of Southold
deceased as followeth Vidlt:

```
Impris. - One house will all the land and meadow......20.00.00
It. - Indean corne....................................10.00.00
It. - 4 cowes.........................................18.00.00
It. - Young cowes.....................................03.00.00
It. - Swine...........................................04.00.00
It. - Beadstead, bead & beding........................05.00.00
It. - The apparell of the decease.....................03.13.00
It. - a parcell of course woollen cloath..............00.18.00
It. - A chest, cradle wth ofther trumpery.............02.17.00
It. - a muskett, sword, & rest........................02.05.00
It. - brasse, puter - with a smoothing iron...........02.05.00
It. - A shovell, tongs - ax - handsawe................00.16.00
It. - two old bibles wth other books..................00.14.00
It. - more lumber in the house........................01.02.00
```

Apprisers underwritten Sworne the day abovesaid.

BARNABAS HORTON
WILLIAM PURRIER
CHARLES GLOVER

Mary the late wife of Peter Payne sworne, that shee
gave in to the Apprisers all her husbands estate.

From Shelter Island:

SUCCESSION OF PROPRIETORS
THE MANHANSETT TRIBE.
THE KING.
THE EARL OF STIRLING.
JAMES FARRETT.
STEPHEN GOODYEAR.
NATHANIEL SYLVESTER.
GILES SYLVESTER.
BRINLEY SYLVESTER.
THOMAS DERING.
SYLVESTER DERING
MARY CATHERINE L'HOMMEDIEU
SAMUEL SMITH GARDINER.
EBEN NORTON HORSFORD.

[On the South Steps.]
Of the sufferings for conscience; sake of friends of
NATHANIEL SYLVESTER,
Most of whom sought shelter here, including
GEORGE FOX,
Founder os the Society of Quakers,
And his followers,
MARY DYER,   MARMADUKE STEVENSON, and
WILLIAM ROBINSON,   WILLIAM LEDDRA,
Who were executed on Boston Common;

[On East Steps.]
LAWRENCE and CASSANDRA SOUTHWICK,
Despoiled, imprisoned, starved, whipped, banished,
Who fled here to die;

[On North Steps.]
DANIEL GOULD, bound to the Gun-carriage and lashed,
EDWARD WHARTON, "The much Scourged."
CHRISTOPHER HOLDER, "The Mutilated,"
HUMPHREY NORTON, "The Branded,"
JOHN ROUS, "The Maimed,"
GILES SYLVESTER, "The Champion"
RALPH GOLDSMITH, "The Shipmaster,"
SAMUEL SHATTUCK, of "The King's Missive,"
THESE STONES ARE A TESTIMONY.

[On West Steps.]
The Puritan in his pride, overcome by the faith of the
Quaker, gave
LEXINGTON AND CONCORD AND BUNKER HILL
TO HISTORY.
The Blood and the Spirit of Victor and Vanquished
alike are the Glory of
MASSACHUSETTS

[On horizontal tablet of a table tomb on Shelter Island]

TO
NATHANIEL SYLVESTER,
FIRST RESIDENT PROPRIETOR
OF
THE MANOR OF SHELTER ISLAND,
UNDER GRANT OF CHARLES II.
A.D. 1666;

[arms]

AN ENGLISHMAN
INTREPID,
LOYAL TO DUTY,
FAITHFUL TO FRIENDSHIP,
THE SOUL OF INTEGRITY AND HONOR,
HOSPITABLE TO WORTH AND CULTURE,
SHELTERING EVER THE PERSECUTED FOR CONSCIENCE' SAKE;
THE DAUGHTERS
OF
MARY AND PHOEBE GARDINER HORSFORD,
DESCENDANTS OF
PATIENCE, DAUGHTER OF NATHANIEL SYLVESTER
AND
WIFE OF THE HUGUENOT BENJAMIN L'HOMMEDIEU
IN
REVERENCE AND AFFECTION
FOR
THE GOOD NAME OF THEIR ANCESTOR
IN 1884
SET UP THESE STONES
1610   FOR A MEMORIAL   1680

[under the table.]

THOMAS BRINLEY King's Auditor, married ANNE WASE
NATHANIEL SYLVESTER   married GRISSELL BRINLEY
BENJAMIN L'HOMMEDIEU   married PATIENCE SYLVESTER
BENJAMIN L'HOMMEDIEU, 2nd   married MARTHA BOURNE
EZRA L'HOMMEDIEU   married MARY CATHERINE HAVENS
SAMUEL SMITH GARDINER   married MARY CATHERINE
L'HOMMEDIEU
EBEN NORTON HORSFORD   married MARY L'HOMMEDIEU GARDINER

93

15th December 1650

The day and year above written I John Tuthill have by these presents, remised, released and forever quitclaimed all my right, title and interest of, in, and unto the Estate of Henry Tuthill my late father deceased, and Bridget Tuthill my mother deceased, and which came into the hands and possession of my now father in law William Wells, by marriage of my said Mother in her life time, and also, all my right and interest unto whatever was given unto me the said John Tuthill by John Tuthill my fathers brother, and was committed to his custody either conditionally or absolutely to my said father in law Wm. Wells and his heirs and assigns forever. And do hereby firmly warrant and defend unto my said father in law against all persons claiming say right or interest, from, and under my estate, right or like

Witness my hand the day and year aforesaid.

                                        JOHN TUTHILL

In the presence of
    John Youngs Pastor
    Marie Wells.   Recorded by me William Wells
                                Recorder for present.

31st May, 1654

Upon some question propounded to the Court concerning Mr. Wells his children, which were Henry Tuthills, of Southold, it is ordered that what evidence can be procured for cleering the childrens portions, should be speedily sent to the Governor, at New Haven the third Wednesday in October next, and if Mr. Wells should remove from Southold, that so much of his estate be securied as may answer, not onely the pportions allready appointed, but also a meete some for that wch may upon evidence further appear to be due to them.

Records from Hartford, Connecticut -

One parcell wch he (Rich Lord) & Wm Gibbons bought of
Captayn Vnderhill wch formerlye did Belonge to ye weft India
Company in North Holland & was Seized by Captaine Jno: Vnderhill
by vertue of a Comifsion Graunted him, Bearing date 24th May:
1653. This parcell lyeth in ye Sowth mead & Containes by
estimation Twenty three Acres & a half (be it more or lefs) &
abutteth on ye land of Capt: Cullett Eaft on ye great river
North on Georg Steels land weft on a highway leading from ye
mead: gate to ye Indian land on ye Sowth

Dated November 29, 1639 document giving "Capt. Jo. Vnderhill"
permission to return to Boston to plead his case:

Whereas, Libertye by letters of Publick Assurceringe such
matters of offence as they had charge him with the time therein
limited beinge longe since expired, I have thought felt (wth
advise & consent of other of the councell) at the earnest
request of th sd Capt. Vnd: to renewe the same & doe hereby
license him to repayer to Boston aforsd, & by verture of the
authoritye & power to myself & the rest of the Councell
Comitted, doe Assure him yt he shall come and returne in peace
& saftty, free from all arests or othere molestation by or from,
any Authoritye heere, he demeaninge himselfe well in his travall
& staye, accordinge to the order of such pck Assurances.

From: Suffolk Deeds, Vol. 1

Below is an abbreviated version of the Vail genealogy given in
<u>Genealogical Tables of the Sovereigns of the World</u>, by Rev.
William Betham of Stonham, Aspwall, Suffolk County, England;
arranged by the Dutchess of Cleveland; printed by William Bennet
of Clement-Inn-Passage, Clare Market, London, in 1795. Assume
the title of each person is the same as the title of the person
above unless a title change has been made, i.e. generation
numbers 1 through 16 are all Kings of the Cimmerians.

VAIL-

Arms - Argent, on a bend sable, three calves passant or.
Crest - A garb or, infiled with a ducal coronet gules.
Motto - Face aut Tace. (Fulfil [sic] and be silent)

Generation	Title	Name	Death Date
1	Kings of the Cimmerians	Antenor I	B.C. 443
2		Marcomir I	B.C. 412
3		Antenor II	B.C. 384
4		Priamus	B.C. 358
5		Helenus I	B.C. 339
6		Diocles	B.C. 300
7		Bassanus	B.C. 250
8		Clodomir I	B.C. 228
9		Nicanor	B.C. 198
10		Marcomir II	B.C. 170
11		Clodius I	B.C. 157
12		Antenor III	B.C. 143
13		Clodomir II	B.C. 121
14		Merodachus	B.C. 93
15		Cassander	B.C. 64
16		Antharius	B.C. 34
17	Kings of the West Franks	Francus	B.C. 1
18		Clodius II	A.D. 20
19		Marcomir III	50
20		Clodomir III	63
21		Antenor IV	69
22		Ratherius	90
23		Richimir	114
24		Odomir	128
25		Marcomir IV	149
26		Clodomir IV	166
27		Farabert	186
28		Huano	213
29		Hilderic	253
30		Bartherus	272
31		Clodius III	298
32		Walter	306
33		Dagobert I	317
34	Dukes of the East Franks	Genebald	350
35		Dagobert II	379
36		Clodius IV	389
37		Marcomir VI	404
38		Pharamond	428
39	King of the Franks	Clodius	455
40	Duke of Moselle	Sigemerus	485
41		Ferreolus	540
42	Margrave of Antwerp	Auspert	570
43	Margrave of Schelde	Arnoaldus	601
44	Saint	St. Arnulf	641

Generation	Title	Name	Death Date
45	Lord of Ansigniers	Anschisus	698
46		Pepin II	714
4		Charles Martel	741
48	King of France	Pepin II	
49	King of France/Emperor	Charlemagne	814
50	Emperor	Louis I	840
51	King of France	Charles II	877
52		Louis II	879
53		Charles III	929
54		Louis IV	954
55	Lord of Ansignieres	Arnould I	
56		Arnould II	1046
57		Gislebert I	1065
58		Gilbertus Le Viele	
59		Ralph La Veyle	
60		Hubert La Veyle	
61	none	Eustace La Veyle	
62		Hubert La Veyle	
64		Peter La Veyle	
65		Galfridus La Veyle	
66		Henry Vele	
67		Robert Vele	
68	Knight of Charfield	Sir Peter Veale	
69		Sir Peter Veale	1385
70		Sir Peter Veale	
71	none	Thomas Vele	
72		John Vele	
73		John Vele	
74		William Vele of Totworth	
75		William Vele of Over	
76		William Vele	
77		Thomas Vele	
78		John Vele of Gloucester	
79		Thomas Vele	
80		John Veale	
81		Jeremiah Vail	1687

Will of Thomas Warren

Thomas Warren of Southwold merchant, 4 March 17th Charles, 1641, proved 13 September 1645. To son Thomas all my houses and lands in Southwold bought of William Burrye late of Muttford and (other houses, tenenments &s.) bought of the Bailiffs of Southwold, sold under the will of Richard Buckenham, with brewhouse &c.. To daughter Elizabeth with of Thomas Gooch of Southwold twenty pounds.

Item, I give and bequeath to the two children of Mary Youngs, my daughter, wife of John Youngs now in New England, the sum of forty pounds EnGlish money, to be paid unto them in manner and form following, i.e. to Mary Gardiner, my said daughter's daughter, the sum of thirty pounds within four years next after my decease. Item, I give unto Benjamin Youngs my grandchild the sum of ten pounds of like English money, to be paid unto him within five years next after my decease. To my daughter Margaret Youngs, the wife of Joseph Youngs, thirty pounds, to be paid ten pounds in six years, ten pounds in seven years and ten pounds in eight years after my decease. To my daughter Christian Barnard, wife of Symon Barnard, twenty pounds, to be paid ten pounds in nine years and ten pounds in ten years after my decease. To my son George Warren ten pounds in eleven years &c. All these sums to be paid by my son Thomas Warren. To my daughter Deborah the house and land in Southwold which I purchased of John Perry and Stephen Herrington. Certain money due from Daniel Stephenson, late of Southwold deceased, to Robert Warren, my son, deceased. Son Thomas and Son in law Simon Barnard to be executors.

Arch. Suff. (Ipswich) Original Wills (1645), No. 120

From the brass tablet in the chancel floor, St. Margaret's
Church, Southwold, England:

> HERE LYETH INTERRED YE BODY OF MR. CHRISTOPHER
> YONGES WHO DEPTED THIS LIFE Y 14 DAY OF IVNE
> ANNO DOMINI, 1626
> A GOOD MAN FVLL OF FAYTH WAS HEE
> HERE PREACHER OF GOD'S WORD
> AND MANIE BY HIS MINISTRIE
> WEARE ADDED TO THE LORD.   (ACT II 24)

Wills of Christopher and Margaret Youngs:

Christopher Yonges, clerk of Southwold, 21 November ____, proved
5 July 1626. To Margaret all aldn &c. for life. Then to my six
children John, Joseph, Christopher, Mary, Margaret and Martha.
To eldest son all my books except some English books such as my
wife or my other children shall choose out for their use, one or
two a piece. To John and Thomas Yonges by grandchildren, to each
a silver spoon. Wife Margaret and John smith and Thomas Eliot of
Southwold to be executors.
                    Consistory Court, Norwich (1626), No. 164

Margaret Youngs late wife of Christopher Youngs deceased of
Southwold, 27 October 1630, proved 8 January, 1630. For the
outward goods that God hath given me I do dispose as followeth.
For the house and land I dwell in I desire it may be divided
amongst my children according to my husband's will. Next for all
mu household stuff &c. belonging to me, my will is, my debts and
funeral charge being paid, the remainder to be equally divided
betwix my six children, John, Joseph, Christopher, Mary,
Margaret, and Martha, or so many as shall be alive at the time
of my decease. My two sons John and Joseph Yonges to be
executors.
                    Arch. Suff. (Ipswich). B.59 (1629-30).
          L.349

A breefe Record of the lands & Meadows pertaineing
to and in the possession of the Inhabitants of the
Towne of Southold.
From 1651 Southold Town Records

1. Mr. John Yongs (Pastor or the forenamed place) his house lott
with the meadow therunto adjoyning is by estemation Seven Acres
more or less, bounded on the North and East with the Street &
Lane, and with the home lott of Robert Akerly West.
2. His home land lying in the old planting field containing five
acres more or less bounded South by ye land of Peter Pain, North
by Samuel Yo. his land.
3. His North Sea lott is be estemation twenty eight acres being
in length 160 pole, lying between the land of William Wells East
and Thomas Mapes West.
4. His land lying on the backside of the Town containing fourty
two acres bounded on ye South by ye land of John Curwin, on ye
north by Joseph Yongs.
5. His land lying in Toms-kreek neck containing eight acres.
6. His twelve acre lott lying at ye reers if ye home lotts on ye
north side ye Towne.
7. His land in ye Calves neck containing four acres more of
less. 8. His good meadow lying and being at Toms-kreek
containing three acres more or less bounded on ye East with the
^R
meadow of Mr. Thomas Moore, on the West by the meadow of John
Curwin.
9. His bad meadow lying at Corchaug containing four acres more
or less, bounded South by ye meadow of Peter Dickerson, north by
Barnabas Horton his meadow.
10. His lott purchased of Abraham Dibell is be estemation four
acres more or less, which sd four acres was formerly Robert
Akerlys, and after...Disbroughs and by him sould to the sd
Dible, and is lying between his own land on ye East, and Mr.
Boots on the West.
11. A tract of meadow lying in Oyster pond lowerneck bounded by
ye land of Charles Glover West, and East by the River.
12. His meadow at Ocquabauck lying on both sides the River.
        His Commanage in the Town bounds is a fourth lott.

From the First Presbyterian Church Cemetery, Southold:

        MR. IOHN YONGS MINISTER OF THE WORD AND FIRST SETLER
    OF THE CHVRCH OF CHRIST IN SOVTHOVLD ON LONG ISLAND
        DECEASESED THE 24 OF FEBRVARY IN THE YEARE
            OF OUR LORD 1671/2 AND OF HIS AGE
        HERE LIES THE MAN WHOSE DOCTRINE LIFE WELL KNOWN
        DID SHOW HE SOUGHT CRISTS HONOVR NOT HIS OWN
            IN WEAKNES SHOWN IN POWER RAISD SHALL BE
            BY CHRIST FROM DEATH TO LIFE ETERNALLY

        The original stone was recut in 1857 by Dea. Stephen
Youngs and Captain Selah Youngs, third and fourth generation
descendants of Rev. John Youngs. It was recut in 1900 by Edward
F. C. Young.

At the Court of Sessions held in Southold for ye East
Rideing of N York Sheir on Long Island, by his Majties authority
in ye eight & twenteth yeare of he reign of our Soveraigne Lord
Charles ye second by the grace of God of great Britian, ffrance
and Ireland, king, defender of the faith &c. and in the yeare of
our Lord God 1675.

Whereas an inventory of ye estate of Mr. John Yongs Pastor
of ye Church of Christ of Southold, deceased, was presented to
ye Court, as also affidavit was made by Mr. Barnabas Wines and
Mr. Barnabas Horton, making faith that ye sd Mr. John Yongs at
or nere his death left all his estate to the sole dispose of his
wife, Mrs. Mary Yongs.

Also shee making sute to the Court for power to administer
of ye said Estate: And haveing put in sufficient standing
security to ye Court according to law in that behalfe these are
to certifie all whome it may concerne that the said Mrs. Mary
Yongs the weidow and relict of him the said Mr. John Yongs
deceased, is by the said Court admitted and confirmed to all
intents & purposes administratrix of all and singular the goods
and chattels and whatsoever Estate or inrest he ye sd Mr John
Yongs died siezed off, or any manner of way rightly appertained
to him: And the said Mrs Mary Yongs hath hereby full power as
administrix to dispose of the said estate or any part thereof as
shee hath occation and the laws of this government alloweth..

In the name and by the order of the Court

Pr me HENRY PERSON Cleark of the Sessions of the East
Rideing.

Inventory of Pastor Young's Estate:

In Wooden war - and 2 old bedsteds - an old chest and
    3 chayers - 2 tables & a forme & boule & tray.....02.00.00
2 Kettles, 2 potts, hake & pothake...................03.00.00
In pewter..02.00.00
2 old beds & boulsters, blankets, one rugg and curtaines
    andveluings......................................04.00.00
lyning and sheets and pillobarrs.....................02.10.00
5 oxen and one alme steir and one cow, and 2 of 2 yeare
    old and one halfe Steere, one yearling............27.10.00
Onehorse...03.00.00
24 sheep...02.00.00
3 small swine..04.00.00
house and Land.......................................30.00.00
Old books - by mr Hubard prised at...................05.00.00

                                                           97.00.00
    BARNABAS WINDS   [sic]
    JOHN CURWIN
    JOSHUA HORTON
    JACOB CORE

Miscellaneous tombstone inscriptions from the Southold, Long
Island area:

HERE LIETH INTERRED
THE BODY OF COLONEL
IOHN YOVNGS ESQUIRE
LATE ONE OF HIS
MAIESTIES COVNCEL OF
THE PROVINCE OF
NEW YORK WHO
DEPARTED THIS LIFE
THE 12 DAY OF APRILL
ANNO DOMINI 1698
AGED 75 YEARS

Here Lyeth Buried
Ye Body of Mary
Vaile Aged 39
Years. Departed
This Life Ye 22
of September
1689

Here lyes Interrd ye
Body of Benjamin
Youngs, Efq. who was
Born in Southold in
Ye Year of our Lord
1668 and Departed
this Life July ye 29th
Anno Domini 1742

Here Lyes Ye Body
Of Mr Jeremiah
Vail Aged 77
Years Decd Novr
Ye 28th 1726

HERE LYES THE
BODY OF MR
JONATHAN TUTHILL
DYED FEBRY 8TH 1741/2
IN YE 50TH YEAR
OF HIS AGE

ERECTED
To the memory of
Nathan Landon
A native of Wales England
Died
March 9, 1718
A.E. 54 ys

Here lyes ye Body
Of Mr BENJAMIN
TUTHILL; Who
Died January 26, 1701
A.E. 30 ys

Here
Lies the
Body of Mr
Annanias Conkling
who died March ye 1
1740 in ye 68 year
of his Age

MARY
CONKLEYN
DECEASED
NOVEMBER 2
1688

Excerpts From The 179 Southold, Long Island Census

Last Name	First Name	Males Over 16	Males Under 16	All Females	Freemen and Slaves	
Bird	William	1				
Brown	David	1		1		
Brown	James	1	5	2		1
Brown	Silvenus	1		4		
Brown	William	1		1		
Brown	Silvenus Sr.	3	2	1	1	
Brown	Sarah				3	
Brown	Thomas	1	1	1		
Brown	Samuel	1	1	1	1	
Brown	Mary			2		
Brown	Rubin	1		1		
Brown	Richard	1	3	2	1	
Brown	Johannah		1	2		
Brown	Absolom	1		5		
Brown	Christopher	2	3		2	
Brown	Richard	1	1	4		
Brown	Mehitibell			1		
Brown	Richard	1	3	4		
Brown	Peter	1	3	1	1	
Conkline	Hannah		2	3		4
Conkline	Thomas	1	3	4	1	
Conkline	Jonathan	1	1	4		1
Conkline	John	1	1	4		1
Conkline	David	1		1	2	2
Conkline	Jonathan	1		5	1	
Conkline	John	1	1	4		
Conkline	Henry	1	2	3	1	
Corvin	Jenning				4	
Corvin	John Jr.	1	1	6		
Corvin	David	3	1	2		
Corvin	John	3		1		5
Corvin	Asa	1	1	1		
Curvin	Daniel	1		3		
Curvin	Richard	1		2	1	
Curvin	Jedediah Jr.	1		1		
Curvin	Jedediah	2		3		
Curvin	Abijah Jr.	1	1	3		
Curvin	Joseph	1		1		
Curvin	Samuel	1	2	3		
Curvin	Silas	3		3		
Curvin	Mary			1		
Curvin	Nathan	1		3		
Curvin	Tithomethy	1		1		
Curvin	Joseph Jr.	1	2	1		
Curvin	Thomas	1	3	3		
Curvin	Stephen	1				
Curvin	Amasiah	1	1	1		
Curvin	Mathias	1		1	1	
Curvin	Jacob	1	2	2	2	1
Curvin	John	2		1	1	
Gardiner	John	1	2	3	1	
Gardiner	Joseph	1		2		
Gardiner	John	3		1	1	4
Hallock	Zachariah	1	2	4		
Hallock	James	1	1	2		
Hallock	Ezerah	1	1		1	

Last Name	First Name	Males Over 16	Males Under 16	All Females	Freemen and Slaves	
Hallock	William	2	5	1		
Hallock	Zebulon	3	1	6		
Hallock	John	2		3		
Hallock	Daniel	1	2	3		
Hallock	Joseph	3	2	3	1	
Hallock	Peter	2		3		
Hallock	Zerubabel	4		3		
Hallock	Zerubabel Sr.	1	2			3
Hallock	William	2	2	1	1	
Hallock	Richard	2	1	5		
Horton	Benjamin	1	4	1	1	3
Horton	Benjamin	2	3	1		
Horton	Jonathan Jr.	1	2	2	1	
Horton	Gilbert	2	1	3	2	1
Horton	Jonathan	1	1	1		2
Horton	Jonathan B.	1	2	2		
Horton	Jonathan Sr.	2	3	3		
Horton	Jonathan	1	1	3		
Horton	William	1		4	1	3
Horton	Joseph	2		2		
Horton	Rebecca	1		4		
Horton	David	4	2	1		
Horton	James	1	1	3	1	
Horton	Joseph	1	1	1		
Horton	Jonathan	1		1	1	
Horton	Joshuah	2	1	3		
Horton	Ambrose	1		2		
Horton	James	1	1	1		
Horton	Mecah	1	1	2		
Horton	William	1	1	1	1	
Landon	Jerrod	2	1	2	1	4
Landon	Mary			1		
Moore	Grovener	1		2		
Moore	Daniel	1	2	2		
Moore	John	3	1	3		
Moore	Simond	1		1	1	
Moore	Hazard	1		2		1
Moore	Zodach	1		3	1	
Moore	Calver	2	1	5		
Moore	Benjamin	1	3	4		
Moore	Abigail	1		3		2
Moore	James	1	2	3	1	1
Moore	Thomas	2	4	5		
Moore	Hannah			3		
Pain	John	1	1	3		2
Pain	John Jr.	1	1	3		
Pain	Benjamin	1		2		1
Pain	Samuel	1	1	3		
Pain	Alsop	1		1		
Pain	John	1		1		
Tuthil	John	1		1		
Tuthil	James	2		2		
Tuthill	Christopher	4		1		
Tuthill	James	1	3	5		
Tuttle	Temperance		1	5		
Tuttle	Jeremiah Sr.	1		1		
Tuttle	Jeremiah Y.	1	1	1		
Tuttle	Ezekiah	1		3		
Tuttle	Daniel	4	2	3		1
Tuttle	Luther	1	2	1		

Last Name	First Name	Males Over 16	Males Under 16	All Females	Freemen and Slaves	
Tuttle	Barnabas	1	1	2		
Tuttle	David	1	1	2		
Tuttle	Samuel	4		2		
Tuttle	Eliza		2	6	1	
Tuttle	John	2	2	3		
Tuttle	Ezeriah	1	1	3	1	
Tuttle	Nathan	2	1	4		
Tuttle	David	1	2	3		
Tuttle	Nathaniel	1	1	4		
Tuttle	John	1	1	2		
Tuttle	Samuel Jr.	1	1	2		
Tuttle	Daniel	1	3	3		
Tuttle	Nathaniel	1	2	4		
Tuttle	Christopher Jr.	1	2	1		
Tuttle	Jeremiah Jr.	2	1	3		
Tuttle	John	1		1		
Tuttle	John	1		1		
Tuttle	Henry	1	1	2		
Tuttle	Rufus	2	3	2		2
Tuttle	Sarah	1		4		3
Tuttle	Patrunes	1		2		
Tuttle	Jonathan	1	2	2		
Vail	Jonathan	2	2	3		
Vail	Elisha	2	1	3		
Vail	Bathiah			1	1	1
Vail	Benjamin Jr.	1		3		
Vail	Nathaniel	1	2	3		
Vail	John	1		1		
Vail	Benjamin	3		2		
Vail	Gillim	1		2		
Vail	Peter	1	5	4		
Vail	Stephen	2	2	3		
Vail	Sebel	1	1	2		
Vail	Peter	1	2	1		
Vail	Sarah		1	2		
Vail	Jeremiah	2		2		
Vail	Obediah	2		2		
Vail	Joshua	1	2	2		
Vail	Thomas	2	4	3		
Yongs	Jonathan	3	2	3		
Yongs	Jeremiah	1	1	1		
Yongs	Thomas	5	1	4		4
Yongs	Betheah			1		
Yongs	Mihitibel	1		2	1	
Yongs	Warren	2	3	6		
Yongs	James	2		4		1
Yongs	Jeremiah	1		1		
Yongs	Nathan	1	1	3		
Yongs	Israel	1	1	1		
Yongs	John	1	2	3		
Yongs	Nathaniel	1	1	2		
Yongs	Daniel	1	2	3		
Yongs	Richard	1	1	1		1
Yongs	Rubin	1	4	4		
Yongs	Daniel	1	1	6		
Young	Thomas	1	3	5	1	
Youngs	Daniel	2	3	5		2
Youngs	Daniel Jr.	1	2	1	1	1
Youngs	John	1				
Youngs	Jeremiah	1	1	1		

Bibliography

Addison, Sir William. Understanding English Place-Names. BT
Balsford, Pub. London. 1978.

Andrews, Charles M. Fathers of New England. United States Bb
N.Y. 1919.

Banks, Charles E. Planters of the Commonwealth: A Study of B
Emigrants & Emigration in Colonial Times. GPC. Baltimore.
1984 Repro of 1930.

Betham, Rev. William. Genealogical Tables of the Sovereigns of
the World. William Bennet. London. 1795.

Bodge, George Madison. Soldiers in King Philip's War. GPC.
Baltimore. 1976 Repro of 1906.

Book of British Towns. Drive Pub., Ltd. Hants, England. 1979.

Browne, John. History of Congregationalism and Memorials of B
Churches in Norfolk and Suffolk. Jarrold and Sons.
London. 1877.

Bunker, Mary Powell. Long Island Genealogies. GPC. Baltimore.
1976.

Calder, Isabel M. New Haven Colony. Shoe String Press. 1970
Repro of 1934.

Campbell, Douglas. Puritans in Holland, England and America.
Harper. 1893.

Case, Albertson. Historical Sketches of Southold Town.
Reprint   by Mary Case Berresford Sinclaire and Sara Case
Faulkner. Date Unknown.

Chidsey, Donald Barr. The Gentleman from New York: A Life of
Roscoe Conkling. Yale University Press. New Haven. 1935.

Clemens, William Montgomery (ed.). American Marriage Records
Before 1699. GPC. Baltimore. 1977.

Crary, Catherine C. The Price of Loyalty. McGraw-Hill Book Co.
New York. 1973.

Cropsey, Joyce MacKenzie (compiler). Register of Revolutionary
Soldiers and Patriots buried in Litchfield   County.
Phoenix   Publishing. Canaan, New Hampshire.   1976.

Essex Institute. Historical Collections, Vols. 1-20. Salem,
Massachusetts. 1859-1883.

French, J.H. Historical and Statistical Gazetteer of New York
State. Heart of Lakes Pub. New York. 1860.

Genealogical and Family History of the State of Connecticut.
Lewis Historical Pub. Co. 1911.

Hartropp, Henry (transcriber). Leicestershire Marriages
Licenses, 1570-1729. British Record Soc., Ltd. 1910.

Hawke, David Freeman. Franklin. Harper & Row. New York. B5

Heads of the Families at the First Census of the United States
    Taken in the Year 1790: New York. Government Printing
    Office. Washington, D.C. 1964 Reprint of 1908.

Hoffman, Edwin. Pathways to Freedom. Houghton Mifflin Co.
    Boston. 1964.

Hutton, Mary Louise Marshall (compiler). Seventeenth Century
    Colonial Ancestors: of Members of the National Society of
    Colonial Dames XVII Century, 1915-1975. GPC. Baltimore.
    1984.

L'Estrange, John (ed.). Calendar of the Freemen of Norwich fim
    1317-1603. Eliot Stock. London. 1888.

Labaree, Leonard W. (ed.). Papers of Benjamin Franklin. Yale
    University Press. New Haven. 1959-69.

Landon, James Orville. Landon Genealogy: The French and
    English Home and Ancestry. Clark Boardman Co., Ltd. New
    York. 1928.

Landon, Truman. "The First Settler" Oliver Landon of Lansdowne.
    Canada. 1979.

Lobdell, Julia Harrison. Nicholas Lobden (Lobdell) - 1635 of
    Hingham, Mass. and Some of His Descendants. 1907.

Lopez, Claude Anne and Eugenia W. Herbert. Private Franklin:
    The Man & His Family. Norton. 1985.

Loyd, Lewis C. The Origins of Some Anglo-Norman Families. GPC
    Baltimore. 1980.

MacKenzie, George. Colonial Families of the United States.GPC.
    Baltimore. 1966.

Mason, Oliver (compiler). Bartholomew Gazetteer of Britain.
    John Bartholomew and Son, Ltd. Edinburgh. 1977.

Michaud, Joseph F. Biographie Universelle Ancienne et Moderne -
    45 Vols. Adlers Foreign Books. 2nd ed. Repro of 1843.

Mires, Dr. Maynard. Short History of the Landon Family in
    America. Village Press. 1978.

New England Historical and Genealogical Register. New England
    Historic Genealogical Society. January, 1848; April, 1849;
    January, 1851; July, 1862; July, 1868; April, 1880; April,
    1923; July, 1925.

Osterweis, Rollin F. Three Centuries of New Haven, 1638-1938.
    Yale Press. New Haven. 1953.

Prevost, M. M. and Jean-Claude Roman D'Amat (eds).Dictionnaire
    de Biographie Francaise. 16 V. French & Eve. France.
    1972.

Roberts, Gary Boyd (ed). English Origins of New England
    Families: From "The New England Historical and Genealogical
    Registry". GPC. Baltimore. 1984.

Roberts, Gary Boyd (ed.) Genealogies of Connecticut Families from "The New England Historical and Genealogical Registry". GPC. Baltimore. 1983.

Rothbard, Murray N. Conceived in Liberty, Vol. 1. Arlington House Pub. New Rochelle, New York. 1975.

Salcorn, Winifred. "Abstracts of the Early Probate Records of New Haven, Book I, Part I, 1647-1687" New England Historical and Genealogical Register. April, 1927.

Savage, James. Genealogical Dictionary of the First Settlers of New England. GPC. Baltimore. No Date.

Scott, Kenneth (compiler). Genealogical Data from Administration Papers from the New York State Court of Appeals in Albany. National Society of Colonial Dames in the State of New York. New York. 1972.

Societe de Gens de Lettres et de Savants. Biographie Universelle Ancienne et Moderne: Histoire, par Order Alphabetique, de la Vie Publique et Privee de Tous les Hommes qui se Sont Fait Remarquer par Leurs Ecrit, Leurs Actions, Leur Talents, Leur Vertus or Leurs Crimes. Chez Madame C. Desplaces. Leipzig. No date.

Sherwood, George. American Colonists in English Records. GPC. Baltimore. 1978.

Starbuck, Alexander. History of Nantucket. C.E. Tuttle Pub. 1969.

Suffolk Co. Wills: Abstracts of the Earliest Wills upon Record in the Co. of Suffolk, Mass. From "The New England Historical and Genealogical Register" (index by Judith McGhan). GPC. Baltimore.

Tepper, Michael. Immigrants to the Middle Colonies: A Consolidation of Ship Passenger Lists & Associated Data from the New York Genealogical & Biographical Record. GPC. Baltimore. 1979.

Tepper, Michael. New World Immigrants. GPC. Baltimore. 1980.

Tepper, Michael. Passengers to America. GPC. Baltimore. 1978.

Thompson, Benjamin F. History of Long Island: From its Discovery and Settlement to the Present Time. Robert H. Dodd. New York. 1918.

Tourtellot, Arthur Bernen. Benjamin Franklin: The Shaping of Genius. Doubleday and Co., Inc. New York. 1977.

Trumbull, Benjamin. Complete History of Connecticut, Civil and Ecclesiastical from It's First Planters from England, in the Year 1630 to the Year 1764. 1972 Repro of 1818 ed.

Trumbull, J.H. and C.J. Hadley (eds.). Connecticut (Colony) Public Records of the Colony of Connecticut (1636-1776). 2 Vols. Hartford. 1850-90.

Van der Zee, Henri and Barbara. A Sweet and Alien Land. Viking Press. New York. 1978.

Venn, John and J.A. (compilers). Alumni Cantabrigienses. University Press. Cambridge, England. 1927.

Virkus, Frederick. Compendium of American Genealogy. GPC. Baltimore. 1968 Repro of 1925.

Waters, Henry F. Genealogical Gleanings in England: Abstracts of Wills Relating to Early American Families with GenealogicalNotes & Pedigrees Constructed from Wills & Other Records, 2 Vols. GPC. Baltimore. 1981   Repro of 1901.

Young, Edward Hudson. Our Young Family in America. Sanborn and Ruth Young, Ruth Young Orb and Helen Young Hardy. Durham, NC. 1947.

www.ingramcontent.com/pod-product-compliance
Lightning Source LLC
Chambersburg PA
CBHW071054280326
41928CB00050B/2503